THE NUMINOUS EFFECT
A Spiritual Journey

JOAN ELIZABETH

THE NUMINOUS
EFFECT

"...Everything can be taken from a man but one thing: the last of the human freedoms – to choose one's attitude in any given set of circumstances, to choose one's own way.

Viktor Frankl
– Man's Search for Meaning

I dedicate this book to all those adult children who grew up in mental illness and substance abuse families. May you have the grace and courage to choose to heal and find your inner freedom.

Contents

JOHN 8:32

INTRODUCTION

I n *Man's Search for Meaning*, Viktor Frankl writes that when
we're no longer able to change a situation, the challenge
is to change ourselves.

In 2005 I was faced with a similar dilemma forcing me
to find an alternative meaning to my life. My catalyst for
change during that period was a lady named Meredith, a
quirky, free-spirited woman who I met through a mutual
friend and who also happened to be a psychologist.

Slowly I began telling my new therapist disjointed pieces
of my childhood and spotty things in my past that didn't
make much sense at the time. As the weeks passed, though,
my confusion turned to alarm, and I grew more and more
unnerved at what came tumbling out of my mouth, hearing
it aloud for the first time in 50 years.

*Was that really how it happened? How could it be? I must
be exaggerating!*

In Meredith's presence, my reality from within was gaining a voice, and now, all I wanted to do was shut it up. In
this self-induced therapeutic process, I had unleashed my

own Pandora's Box of emotions and wanted but didn't know how to seal it back up.

I imagined a mock tribunal attended by my father, brother, and sister sitting in Meredith's office listening to what my new-found voice had to say.

Daddy would shake his head and blame me for not loving my mother, echoing her lasting portrayal of me as a liar.

My little brother Timmy would laugh and crack a joke or two, disassociating himself from the family dynamics.

And my older sister Cathleen would quietly sit in the corner, neither denying nor acknowledging what went on in the family.

None of them would see my perspective. And as the realization of that truth slowly set in, I began feeling like a rudderless ship heading into deeper, more turbulent waters.

Meredith sensed my inner desolation when I brought up snippets of the relationship I had with my parents, particularly my mother. At the time, I had moved back home and was living with my widowed mother, medicating my pain with a couple of bottles of Bordeaux, stopping only when the heartburn and hot flashes worked together to make my drinking unbearable.

At 50 years old, I was talking trash about my parents to a stranger, a therapist, and a Jew. Directly violating my Irish Catholic roots that taught the Fourth Commandment of "Honor thy Father and Mother" was as sacred as Jesus Christ himself.

In one of our earlier sessions, Meredith mentioned Viktor Frankl's book, and out of curiosity, I bought a copy.

At first glance, I thought, "Oh, here we go, another book on the Holocaust, another rant about being a victim. Wah, wah, wah. Oh, poor me! Pour me another drink. Suck it up! It's the past, that's what my people taught me to do."

Logotherapy was a term Frankl created for finding purpose and meaning in life after surviving but losing his loved ones to the Nazi death camps. At the time, logotherapy sounded more like the imagination of some Madison Avenue ad jock and not a word crafted for existentialism in the 1940s.

However, as I pressed on, my inner philosopher and feminine Freud became intrigued by the author's observation of the human condition, especially his description of how people behave in captivity and what the psychological effects of long-term deprivation and imprisonment had on the body, mind, and soul.

Based on his observations, Frankl concluded those prisoners less damaged by incarceration were sensitive souls who nurtured an inner life. They were men and women who, before their captivity, lived in a rich intellectual world of their own making, whether it was music, art, literature, or a love of something beyond themselves. Having a passion for something or someone outside of themselves sustained them during the daily uncertainty of death and the unspeakable mental and physical suffering they endured.

"They were able to retreat from their terrible surroundings to a life of inner riches and spiritual freedom," Frankl wrote.

"In some way, suffering ceases to be suffering the moment it finds meaning, such as the meaning of a sacrifice," he wisely noted.

My family legacy is a spiritual one, composed of secrets, alcoholism, and 60's Catholicism, the trifecta in human affliction and oppressive trinity of its time. Any one of these maladies might have caused significant disruption in other families. In mine, it kept us together.

Meredith used the term, *post-traumatic stress disorder,* or PTSD in one of our sessions when I told her pieces of my past that made no sense to me. She said my parents set me up to fail. I hated her for saying such a thing, but deep down, I knew she was right. There was little evidence to suggest otherwise.

I told her I wanted to write a book, to be an author, a dream harbored in some safe portal in my soul, but one that was slowly drifting into obscurity and old age. She responded by calling me resilient, comparing me to a water lily flourishing in the desert terrain. I lived for weeks on that mental sketch, knowing it was a therapeutic mirage but one that certainly eclipsed anything positive I could say about myself at the time.

As if on cue, Meredith's three-year-old poodle, Buttons, jumps up on the leather couch beside me. I stroked the dog's brown curly fur for as long as he allowed. I came to believe that Buttons was part of the healing process. Sometimes I'd get annoyed by the animal's presence, wanting to push the dog off the couch so I could have Meredith all to myself. Other times, all I wanted to do was lie still, close my eyes, and cherish the safety that these surroundings afforded me for the 50 minutes.

Meredith was kind, nurturing, and never pressured me about my drinking. And I thrived in this supportive, therapeutic environment. My experience in 2005 was the beginning of putting the pieces of my fragmented life together, one that was long overdue in being examined and put into its proper perspective.

Frankl's prisoner-of-war persona played in my head, conjuring up the psychological fetters my 60's childhood shared with his world in the 1940s. My upbringing was a carelessly constructed environment, breeding a victim-survivor mentality. Those of us without any power were at the mercy of the one who had most of it.

For me, it was my mother, a woman who kept her darkest secrets to herself and shared nothing with anyone. She was the Irish matriarch who had her own arbitrary rules for the game of life, and it was my job, along with the rest of the family, to figure out what those rules were and obey them.

In Frankl's world, Mommy was the 'Capo,' the camp captain. The victim turned victimizer.

Daddy was the kinder, more sympathetic of my two parents. He would be the friendly but weak SS guard, who would have been over the Capo, but in my world, his parental power and authority subordinated my mother's.

Yes, there were random acts of kindness throughout my childhood, keeping me hopeful for more. But the expectation of any consistent generosity of thought, word or deed was never guaranteed, and most certainly couldn't be demanded, because then it would never come. Even a child's best ally, obedience, couldn't ensure adult benevolence.

Degradation was best saved for the public, times when a neighbor came over to share a beer with my dad. It was then that my sister Cathleen or I got blindsided into being the brunt of an adult joke.

Pointing to my non-existent breasts at 13, Daddy would say in front of our neighbor 'Uncle' George that I should go to the gas station to get my flats fixed. And from time to time, my overweight sister was reminded that clothes cost more at Lane Bryant for girls her size.

Of my two parents, Daddy was the stable force, the breadwinner, the one who provided *a roof over our heads*. It was a phrase Mommy often used, reminding us how grateful we should be for that roof.

When he wasn't cracking jokes at our expense, Daddy made us laugh by making funny faces and singing silly songs. His attentiveness toward his daughters depended on Mommy and her moods. Some days, if Cathy or I claimed too much of his time and affection, or were having too much fun with him, she would grow silent and sullen. Other days, she didn't seem to mind. If Mommy's moodiness ever got pointed out, she would get angry and vehemently deny it, as she did most things. That's why nothing ever changed.

Alcohol was the elixir used to remedy our family's unhappiness, a silent discomfort no one dealt with, but we all endured like an unwanted trip to the dentist.

The world my parents created for their children came wrapped in 60s Catholicism, a religion obsessed with the hereafter. We were mind-locked into believing the afterlife was the only life, and that whatever sufferings and abuse we endured here on earth was worth the price of admission to heaven.

Death and preparing our soul for such was the primary goal. There was no room in my religion to understand who we were. The self was selfish and considered sinful, and thinking outside of the confessional box was unthinkable.

My idea of mental illness has changed over the years. It's not as straightforward or conventional as someone who hears voices, chases butterflies with a net, or sits in some dark corner sucking their greasy hair. Society has gotten more complicated and less institutionalized, and so have the labels in the mental health field.

Diagnostic labels like borderline, sociopathic, or narcissistic personality disorder don't help much. The people who merit these psychiatric tags don't seek help and are certifiable only to those who intimately know them.

I've come to realize that some mental conditions aren't organic but originate from a form of deception within the family structure. I believe the seed of my own disorder was rooted in such confusion, in what was the truth and what wasn't.

So embedded was this collective lie within my family that the power of its shame kept me complicit for much of my adult life, creating in me a vacillating, chameleon-like personality.

In 1982 I married a man whose shame was so deep-ly-rooted within himself that he artfully passed it down to our children like some mangled heirloom from the family attic.

Believing that I could escape my childhood pain through marriage was an illusion. I had traded one falsehood for another. And to be truly free, I would have to understand my life as a whole. I would have to question and grapple with everything I knew and was taught, including my religion and the identity my parents gave me that I wasn't significant enough for them to love.

During one of our therapy sessions, I asked Meredith, "Do you think we're called upon to save others in this life?"

She wasn't surprised by the question. Apparently, there were plenty of other modern-day prisoners-of-war sitting on her couch, stroking her poodle, and reading Viktor Frankl.

"Joan, the only person we're obligated to save is our self."

I groaned inwardly. It wasn't the answer I wanted to hear. My sweet, naïve therapist didn't seem to understand that *self* was a foreign concept in my world. I had grown up without a sense of self, relying on others to define and stroke my shaky self-image.

The problem now is that the world I once knew was gone, destroyed in the aftermath of family dysfunction. I had to find a new way to live. If what Meredith said was correct, that I needed to save myself, it was terrifying to think of focusing just on me. The thought of trying to redefine my life at this late stage sent me into a tailspin of fear.

"Think not that I come to send peace on earth: I come not to send peace, but a sword, for I come to set a man at variance with his father, and the daughter against her mother. And a man's foes shall be they of his own household."

MATTHEW 10:34-36

THE SANDCASTLE

M
y hands feel clammy clenching the steering wheel of our 1990 Ford station wagon. Except for the distant whiff of a happy meal lingering in the backseat, the Taurus still has that new, fresh-car smell to it.

As I pull away from the driveway, I glance back in the rear-view mirror at the two empty car seats reserved for my seven-year-old twins, Brian and Brendan.

It reminds me of their earlier whining on why they couldn't go with me to Grandma and Poppy's house. Latching onto my pant leg, the two of them sing-song, 'Why can't we go?' until the promise of a surprise when I get back quiets them down.

Mary, our 14-year-old babysitter, drew their attention away from the front door, allowing me to leave. The boys are gaga over Mary, who is also a twin, and she smiles, knowing the impish hold she has over them. She tells me not to worry. It's comforting to know my children are in good hands until I return.

My heart and mind are racing simultaneously at seeing my father. The narrow, one-lane winding road between my parent's house on City Island and mine in New Rochelle is a convenient 15-minute drive away. Today, I wish it were longer. I want this same road that connects lower Westchester County to the Bronx to be washed out by rain, closed due to construction, a car accident, anything that will prolong the uncertain outcome of this self-imposed trip, or should I say, self-imposed trap.

I rehearse over and over in my head what I want to say to my dad, but nothing sounds right. Despite all the openness of today's talk shows, I find no script for this, no easy way to tell my father he molested me fifteen years ago at the age of 21.

As I drive closer to my destination, I feel less confident, convinced that what I have to say to him will make me look ridiculous instead of understood. I pull into the gas station, relieved to find another car in front of me, delaying the inevitable for another few minutes.

The first time I heard an inner voice say, *tell your father what he did*, I thought I'd lost it, that this was the beginning of schizophrenia or that imaginary butterfly chase. At the time, I was praying the rosary for comfort and guidance on what to do about my husband Bill's drinking problem. Without warning, a voice spoke to me. I was ill-prepared for what it had to say, much less the authoritative tone it took. It was an uncomfortable command dredging up an incident best left locked in the family's skeleton closet.

I wasn't sure if what I heard was demented or divine, but it was persistent, demanding I confront my father. Like some ghost haunting my dreams, the command stayed with me for months, penetrating my daily thoughts, prayers, and sleep. I finally gave in, saying what the hell, convincing myself that telling my father might be a good thing, opening up the possibility of a clean father-daughter slate between us.

"Ten dollars regular, please. Oh, and check the oil too," I tell the gas station attendant, hoping to buy more time.

Once again, I notice the two empty car seats in the rearview mirror, reminding me how things have changed since I was a kid. Back in the 60s, the ride home from my grandparent's house on Sunday nights could be hazardous. My sister Cathy and I sat in the back hatch of the Pontiac Tempest swaying to and fro from Daddy's sudden turns. There were no car seats or seat belts back then, but we kept a blanket and pillow in the station wagon, shielding our heads from the bumpy ride home.

Holding baby Timmy in her lap, Mommy would be yelling from the passenger seat telling Daddy to slow down, especially on those icy winter nights when the hill on 233rd Street could be treacherous. On those nights, Mommy said we got home *on a wing and a prayer.*

No one talked about the hazards of drunk driving back then. And definitely, no one in my family brought it up the next day. It was a weekly Sunday nightmare that we treated as a figment of our imaginations.

I'm relieved to have given birth to boys and not girls, not because males are superior as my mother and many in her generation believe. If I had twin girls, even one daughter, I'm not sure what I could teach her about the world, or what she could expect outside the roles of being a daughter, wife, and mother.

This is where my own female identity gets murky. I'm vaguely aware of the empty hole, that space inside me that needs nurturing and definition, but I don't know how to change, how to transform it. Maybe today's encounter with my father will fill in some of that troubling space.

What do I call this thing I'm doing today -- an intervention, an act of love, a path toward salvation, or just plain crazy?

⚬

When I recall that night in 1975, sometimes I rationalize it and tell myself it was no big deal. It happened just once. Other times, I'm aware it left a scar because I can't seem to forget the trauma.

Daddy was drunk. He had what I believe to be an *alcoholic blackout*, a term I recently heard about in my weekly Al-Anon meetings. A blackout from alcohol is like having temporary amnesia. Although the person is awake and appears conscious, they have no memory of what was said or what they did when drunk.

Back then, my father spent most of his weekends in the basement tinkering with some new gizmo, listening to music and drinking beer. He spent hours in his workshop doing dad things, fixing something in the house, mowing the lawn, or changing the oil in his car.

A door inside the basement led to the garage, where he housed the new Buick after trading in the Pontiac. My father was a meticulous man, a natural-born mechanic, the kind of guy who wouldn't drive out of the garage unless the car had a tune-up, a fresh oil change, and was buffed spotlessly clean. He kept his countless tools systematically hung on grooved pegboard over his workbench, organizing and sorting even the smallest of items like nails, screws, and lug nuts into glass jars or in a red metal cabinet.

On many weekends, there was loud music playing over the drilling and banging, songs reflecting his mood. Sometimes it was country blues, and other times big band music.

The basement was my father's refuge, his man cave, and most times where he stayed until the call from the top of the stairs came.

"Billy, shut that shit off and come up and eat!"

I was 21 years old and had been living on my own for about a year and a half. Someone broke into the apartment I was renting, and though there wasn't much worth stealing, the incident shook me up. My mother felt sorry for me and said, for the time being, I could move back home.

I looked at the gesture as a fresh start between my parents, especially my father, because he's the one who accused me of being 'just like my sister' and told me I had to move out. I'm home barely six months on the night it happened.

Daddy and I are sitting at the kitchen table. I'm working on a crossword puzzle, and he's watching something on the portable television.

My father is a difficult man to know. When he isn't drinking, he's quiet and reserved. When he drinks, he's approachable. As I see it, getting a second chance at having a father-daughter relationship is up to me.

Daddy's a history buff who likes to read and watch documentaries on television. I need something we can share, something that makes us bond, so I take up crossword puzzles with historical themes.

It's late, past ten on a Sunday evening. I have work the next day. Mommy has gone upstairs to her bedroom. Daddy spent the day in the basement drinking beer. Now the two of us are sitting across from each other at the kitchen table.

Knowing the Monday morning commute into Manhattan can be stressful, I'm anxious to go upstairs and get ready for bed. But I also want to finish the last of this crossword puzzle. So I ask my father if he knows the answer to one final clue. He shuts the TV off and tells me to bring the book around the table so he can have a better look.

I do as he says and lean over him, pointing to the page. He puts his hand on his leg and tells me to sit on his lap.

What an odd request.

The last time I sat on his lap, I was maybe eight or nine. Being asked at 21 feels awkward and out of place, but I chalk it up to his lame attempt of finally trying to connect with his daughter. Perhaps this is his way of telling me he's sorry for throwing me out, making me leave home at such an early age with only a high school education.

I try to ignore the smell of sour beer on his breath, concentrating on this rare moment my father has bestowed on me. My right arm is around his neck, trying not to put my full weight on his legs, and I place my left arm on the table for support.

I feel his hand guiding my chin from the puzzle page to his face. I'm taken aback by the kiss on the lips. And am now terrified by the tongue prying its way into my mouth. I start to panic. My body tenses up. Nanoseconds of thoughts flash through my brain on what I should do.

Should I slap him? Should I stab him with my pencil? Or, should I just let him?

I stare at him wide-eyed, but his eyes remain closed. I feel sick and want to vomit. I push him away, run upstairs, and lock the bedroom door behind me.

The next morning he's in the kitchen making coffee.

"Want a cup?" he asks.

I stare at him, looking for any trace, some evidence of guilt or shame on his face. There is none. He sits at the table, sipping his coffee and reading the newspaper as is his habit.

I'm confused, stunned, and scared.

Overnight, my father has become a stranger. From that day on, I will have panic attacks whenever I'm alone with him in the same room.

Now 15 years later, driven by a persistent inner voice to open up this can of worms, I'm hopeful that once the news is out, my father will apologize, I can heal, and we can all move forward.

I want a healthy relationship with my dad, one that won't interfere with the thriving one he now has with his grandsons and my husband. So I'm ready, willing, and able to accept an apology, to forgive and forget. I want this over. I want a new beginning.

I make the left on City Island Avenue and drive up the block to my parent's house. The Buick is in the driveway, a sign that my father is home. I take one last drag from my menthol cigarette, hoping to alleviate the sheer terror clutching at my heart. My armpits are sweating, and my head is pounding.

I feel the urge to drive away, but remind myself I told them I was coming at noon. When Ma asked why the unexpected visit, I'm vague, piquing her interest even more.

Walking up the front steps, I hold onto the wrought iron railing for support. Obeying this voice inside my head now feels like a death knell. Joan of Arc I'm not and my reflection in the Plexiglas door confirms it. The distorted image of myself highlights how twisted this whole idea now seems.

Mother looks through the peephole before opening the door. She knows it's me, but she's a creature of habit. She greets me as though she just let in the dog. My heart is racing. Her lack of interest wouldn't bother me on any other day, but now it only amplifies how crazy this all seems. I need some encouragement, a sign that what I'm about to do is the right thing. There is none.

What the hell am I doing here? Why did I have to listen to some crazy-ass voice in my head?

I feel the need to run, but it's too late. Daddy's sitting at the kitchen table, in the same chair he did 15 years ago, smoking a cigarette and drinking coffee.

I glance at my watch – 11:58.

Crap, I'm two minutes early!

The smell of cigarette smoke makes me want one, but I'm afraid to show how nervous I am. I tell myself I should be able to talk to my parents about anything, but who am I kidding?

I know if I don't say this with love and confidence, they'll misunderstand my intention. If I stutter my words, they'll eat me alive. I want my father to understand that my motive is not to hurt him but only to get the truth out.

"Daddy, I have something to say to you."

Oh, God, not a good start. He knows that, you halfwit. You can see it on his face!

He looks up from reading the newspaper.

"Yes?" His eyebrows furrow in response.

"I love you, Daddy, you know that. But something has been on my mind for a long, long time."

The words rush from my mouth so much faster than I want or even thought possible.

"When I was 21, you molested me here at the kitchen table."

My mother's arms are elbow deep in the kitchen sink, washing leftover dishes from breakfast. Her back is toward me, but when she hears what I say, she swoops around with raptor-like ferociousness, leaving a spray of water in her wake.

"What the hell did I just hear? That your father molested you? Why you're a goddamn liar!"

"No, no, I'm not Ma," I say calmly. "Daddy was drunk. He started kissing me and put his tongue inside my mouth."

"Ohhh? So what's a little tongue?" she snipes.

Dear Mother of God! What the hell did I do? What am I doing here?

Without thinking, I blurt out, "Daddy molested Cathleen too, in Edgewater. I know Grandpa did it to me when I was eight. He put his hand up my dress and rubbed my thigh after giving me a dollar for candy."

"Why you goddddammmmn fucking liar!" she hisses.

Terrified at the glaring hatred in her eyes, I step back, expecting to get slapped across the face.

"If it's true, why didn't you say something sooner?" she screams. "Why are you telling me this now?"

"I wasn't planning on telling you about grandpa, but it's true. Cathleen said grandpa did the same thing to her."

"Oh, that one, that sister of yours, she's nothing but a fucking liar too! What makes *you people* think you're so goddamn special that your grandfather would do something like that?"

"I didn't feel special, Ma. I felt used. After a few times, whenever he came into the living room with his dollar bill, I ran the other way."

While dodging her flailing arms and jarring accusations, I look over at my father. I can't tell from the stoic look on his face whether he's struggling with what he just heard or doesn't give a shit.

Was I right, had he been in an alcoholic blackout? I wonder if he remembers anything about that night.

"I wanted Daddy to know that ever since it happened, I've been afraid to be alone with him in the same room."

In this unbearable juncture of silence, when she's staring at me bug-eyed, and he's just casually smoking a cigarette, I meekly mouth something about wanting us all to heal as a family.

Oh God, how lame!

My mother screams, "Heal what, for Chrissake? Does anyone else in the family know about this?"

Before I can respond, she points to the door. "Get the hell out of my house."

"Ma, I honestly wasn't saying this to hurt anyone. I just wanted the truth to come out." My eyes fill with tears.

She grabs me by the shoulders, spins me around, and pushes me out the front door. "Get the hell out, and don't ever come back!"

Estrangement was that shaky precipice I stood on for most of my life, a finely-tuned emotional tactic my mother used to threaten and control the family. The ever-present menace of maternal abandonment loomed over us like a genetic form of cancer, creating an early schism within the family fabric. To avoid her critical comments and disapproving nature, everyone, including my father, found a way to survive.

My father's silence and my mother's pointed rage pushed me off the cliff that day. Listening to and acting upon that inner voice sent me headlong into a dark abyss of anger and confusion.

Ideally, the encounter was supposed to be about a father and daughter healing the past, and that's how I convinced myself to do it. It could've been simple. It wasn't supposed to turn out to be such a fiasco, and it certainly wasn't supposed to be about my mother. But in hindsight, I should've known better. It was *always* about her.

Most times, I was aware of the invisible shield between us. I instinctively knew my mother's selfish nature prevented any genuine nurturing. As a kid, I prayed never to get a life-threatening disease, one that required a deeper level of care other than the food, clothing, and shelter I did receive. Childhood fantasies of testing her maternal love created a lot of anxiety, making me cringe at my dark, uncomfortable thoughts.

In my TB scenario, I imagined myself coughing and wheezing for days, months at a time, waiting by the sanitarium window for my mother to come, but she never does. In another, I get stricken with polio and envision how impatient she would get because I was taking too long to reach the bathroom on my crutches. But the most terrifying scenario was the kidnapping plot where she neither cried nor pleaded on the six o'clock news for her beloved Joanie to return, no matter what the ransom.

The intense vulnerability I felt around my mother's indifference never went away but eventually subsided as I got older and could disengage from whatever dependence I had on her.

But today, I inadvertently created the most vulnerable situation that could exist between a mother and daughter. The day presented an opportunity for her to turn all those hurtful, dispassionate years around with just a glance of protective compassion, a sympathetic word, or even a sharp look at my father asking him if my accusation was true. Instead, the last thing I saw was the hate in her eyes.

My head is pounding, and white noise is swirling in my brain. I sit in the car outside my parent's house, trying to shake loose what just happened. Unable to find the strength to turn the key in the ignition, I fumble for a cigarette to calm my nerves.

The living room blinds move, a sign that eyes are peeking out to see if I've gone. I know my mother's thoughts. If I'm parked too long, I will draw the attention of our next-door neighbor, Jack, who's working under the hood of his car. He's waving at me now, and I can feel the pressure from the vapid eyes behind the blinds to leave before he comes over to ask if anything's wrong.

As I drive away, relieved to be heading home to the safety of my own family, I imagine the wind up of this tumultuous day in the kitchen.

My parents will shake their heads in dismay, wondering if my brother and sister know anything about it, or if I told anyone else outside the family. My mother will take the whiskey bottle out and pour each of them a stiff drink.

The very thing that created this confrontation will be used to squash it. Alcohol is the family's liquid referee; a third-party mediator used to calm the inner turmoil before it can rise to the surface and strike inside the family ring.

There will be no questions asked of my father if what I said was true. Nor will he comment on my mother's extreme reaction. They'll shake their heads in righteous indignation, wondering how their daughter could lie about such an awful thing.

Afterward, my father will go upstairs and take a nap, and my mother will do a load of laundry before getting dinner ready.

The incident in the kitchen would sum up my parent's 40-year marital bond of 'Don't Ask, Don't Tell,' a philosophy of theirs, long before it became a military slogan.

THE EARLY MOSAIC YEARS

The year is 1960, a period in time when no working-class family understood the human psyche, nor did they wish to delve into it. It's a black and white world with very little gray. Some might call it a simpler age when fathers worked hard to obtain the American Dream of homeownership, and mothers anchored that home with domesticity for the sake of their children.

It's a time when people cared more about what their neighbors would say or think, than what the underbelly of humanity was doing inside the walls of that dream.

I am six-going-on-seven when the family leaves Brooklyn, and we move to Edgewater Park in the Bronx. Cathleen is eight, and Timmy is still in the womb. My parents have been married for ten years, and Mommy is pregnant for the last time. Any memories I have before we leave Brooklyn come from a Brownie Hawkeye with black and white photos of shirt-tail relatives that I'll rarely see after we move.

Daddy graduates night school that year and gets a job with the City of New York as a heating and air conditioning mechanic, making him enough money for a down payment on our first house. Mommy is glad. She never liked Brooklyn and wants to be closer to her parents, who live in the same house she grew up in, an Irish immigrant neighborhood called Wakefield in the North Bronx.

Daddy's family still lives in the South Bronx, a place they continue to call home long after my grandfather dies. This part of the borough is an ever-changing neighborhood where Daddy locks the car door and holds my hand tight when we walk up the five flights of stairs to visit his mother.

The Bronx is where the memories begin, and Edgewater is the place where the multi-colored stones of the family mosaic get placed before me. Edgewater will create the outer corners of my genealogical puzzle, one that will take several decades to fill in and understand how all the pieces fit together.

The term *tight-knit* is literal for Edgewater Park, a self-contained beach community with its hundreds of shanty bungalows pressed and clustered together along the backdrop waters of the Long Island Sound.

The Park has no sidewalks, and the compressed streets only allow for one car to go up or down the block at any given time.

The home addresses contain both numbers and letters, identifying families mostly by the lettered section. We live in B Section, three blocks from the water.

Daddy buys a brown wooden bungalow with bright yellow window frames. At some point, he'll remove the shingles and put up light blue aluminum siding and re-paint the sashes white. A home project that most of our neighbors will admire, and some will imitate.

Like many in Edgewater, we are a paycheck to paycheck family. And the empty coffee cans lined along the kitchen shelf labeled for specific purposes such as -- house, car, insurance, and school tuition -- are daily reminders of our economic status.

Exchanging clothes between neighbors is common, and hand-me-downs are the norm for anyone with two or more kids of the same sex. Getting new clothes and shoes comes at Christmas, Easter, and birthdays, or when one of us makes the sacraments of Holy Communion and Confirmation.

When Daddy gets paid on Friday, he fills up the car's gas tank and buys himself a case of beer. The beer is his reward for being the breadwinner, and filling up the gas tank ensures he'll continue in that role.

Mommy counts out the remaining cash and puts a couple of five and ten dollar bills into the designated coffee cans. Whatever is left is spent on food. After she asks a neighbor to babysit Timmy, the four of us pile into the Pontiac and head toward the A&P for our weekly rations.

Cathleen and I are allowed to choose five cans of soda, and the 'five cans for a dollar' must last until the following Friday. Choosing the flavors is one of the few liberties we have.

Mommy flirts with the butcher, hoping he might throw in a free piece of beef liver with the usual pound of chuck chop she uses for meatloaf. Sometimes he obliges, but as I see it, it's a good week when the butcher shakes his head saying he doesn't have anymore. It means no liver and onions and getting spared Daddy's 'brain food' speech and corresponding eye gesture that a few more wouldn't hurt.

We eat dinner as a family, but in silence, so the focus is what's on the plate. Whether its meatloaf, pork chops, chicken legs, or the dreaded liver and onions, it's always served with mashed potatoes from scratch and canned corn or peas. Whatever's on the menu is dry and tasteless, and we have milk to wash it down. No one leaves the dinner table without finishing the meal, and no one makes a face.

Sometimes, Daddy, who professes to be 'the best cook in the 88th division,' steps up to make his famous chipped beef with egg noodles. The meat is moist and goes down effortlessly. When Daddy cooks, he usually bakes an apple pie from scratch - a skill he also learned being in the service. We are all happy on nights when chipped beef and apple pie are on the menu and use our glass of milk to toast our father's culinary skills.

Edgewater Park has its own set of stores and a volunteer fire department. We live down the block from the firehouse, which is the social hub for parades, parties, and patriotism throughout the year. The holidays of Memorial Day, July 4th, and Labor Day get celebrated in a flurry of red, white, and blue flags, along with community barbecues, and competitive water and running races sponsored by the Park's athletic association.

On Halloween, kids and grownups alike, dress up for the annual ragamuffin parade, giving prizes out for the best costume. Afterward, we go house-to-house trick or treating, and no one turns us away.

Even Thanksgiving is fun when the volunteer fire department lets us sit on the firetruck, and the firemen hand out vanilla and chocolate ice cream cups, and we can have as much as we want.

Our little beachfront community reflects the values of God, country and family, similar themes that I see acted out on nightly television shows like "Leave it to Beaver," "Andy Griffith," and "Ozzie and Harriet."

It's a time and place when my world and the one I see on television gives me a sense of continuity, believing in the innate goodness of myself and those around me.

As a self-sustaining community, no one ever has to leave Edgewater to get what they need. It has a bakery, deli, dry cleaner, barber, beauty salon, candy store, shoemaker, hardware and stationery store, as well as a gas station all located in the center of the Park.

I know all the store owners, and they know me. Mrs. Barnes, whose family owns the hardware store, is also my Girl Scout troop leader who guides me toward my first two badges in cooking and reading.

Bluebird Bakery serves up freshly baked loaves of pumpernickel, rye and onion bread; bread that bears no resemblance to the white Wonder kind we have in our lunchbox every day at school. Sunday is the bakery's busiest day. It's when the after-Mass crowd gets their patience tested waiting in line with a ticket, hoping there will be enough fresh rolls, donuts, and layer cakes available when their number finally gets called.

Mindful of our obligation to abstain from meat on Fridays, a German-owned deli caters to our predominantly Catholic neighborhood by keeping an extra supply of fish cakes, potato, and macaroni salads on hand.

For obvious reasons, the candy store is the most popular with the kids in town. The five-cent deposit from returning your father's empty beer bottles could be lucrative and buy a week's supply of penny candy and a Spaldeen from the local mom and pop store. This same convenience store is where husbands buy their cigarettes and newspaper before catching the bus to work, and kids get sent with a folded note and return home with a box of Kotex wrapped in brown paper and string for their mothers and sisters.

In the '60s, Edgewater Park is a child's paradise. For me, it's a Garden of Eden, one that's filled with tarred bumpy roads and sandy beaches, ripe with the promise of living each day in the present moment.

Each section of the Park has a separate little beach offering some unique swimming feature -- a diving board, floating jetty, or sliding pond -- all designed to ward off boredom and sharpen a kid's swimming skills. The beach is where I learn to swim underwater, believing I can exist as a mermaid until my lungs scream otherwise.

With a piece of window screen, some bakery cord, and a stale slice of bread, I spend hours minnow fishing off the pier, watching them wiggle for their life before throwing them back into the water. Piss clams and horseshoe crabs get dug up, pinched, and swung as weapons against the local boys in playful summer recess.

There is no end to summer adventures as long as a kid obeys the once-a-day check-in rule, which usually means going home for a quick lunch of peanut butter and jelly sandwiches and chocolate milk.

There's always someone outside to play with, but most times, it's with my friend Richie, who lives a few doors down. Richie and I take turns playing on a make-shift tree swing in one of the vacant lots and have slingshot fights with squares of linoleum tiles as ammunition.

On hot, humid nights, grownups sit on the stoop drinking beer and smoking cigarettes watching their kids get in the last hours of daylight with a spirited game of Johnny on the Pony. Long after we go inside for our nightly bath, the adults stay out past midnight laughing and telling jokes they don't want their kids to hear.

In winter, when heavy snows close the schools, the community comes alive with creativity. Competition for the best snowman or snow family is fierce and unforgiving in what an Edgewater-ite will do to outshine and sabotage his neighbor. Clothes, hats, scarves, and other gimmicks get used to adorn the short-lived snow figures, and some encourage their dogs to pee on the competition's work of art.

When temperatures drop below zero, the fire department hooks up a hose to the hydrant and fills a vacant lot with water creating a make-shift ice rink, and this is where I learn to ice skate.

Most of my childhood adventures involve a second-hand Schwinn, which I paint the same avocado green as our kitchen cabinets. I'm proud of mastering the wheelie, eventually riding downhill without holding onto the handlebars. I'm most proud of buying the bike from the money I made running errands. For $5.50, the bike came with two flat tires, a bent wire-mesh basket, and a rusty bell.

I have a natural talent for running and do it every chance I get. I move as fast as I can everywhere I go, running from the house to the store, with the dog, over the hedges, to the beach or up a tree – all in my white soiled Keds. There's something ethereal and wing-like when I run. I jump, hop, skip or vault with strength and speed, -- better than any boy on the block, or so I believe. Some days I can sprout wings, and in my sleep, the dreams of those wing-like possibilities come alive. It's in that marvelous twilight imagery that I can fly past the limitations of something I have no conscious words to describe. In my dreams, I am the Nike goddess before they made a shoe out of her.

I live in a time when older people are valued, and children have a fearful respect for their elders. We're obliged to offer our youthful services to shovel their snow or rake leaves for them. It's a good day when old Mrs. Savage, with her crooked arthritic finger, dips into her change jar and pulls out a quarter like a fish on a hook. There's no guarantee of the coveted quarter, but the reassurance of being a good girl gets compensated with a pat on the head.

Being obedient gives us leverage with the grownups, who are all looked upon as authority figures. Any kid caught stealing, lying or fighting, permits a parent or another adult to correct the wrong-doer, even if it means slapping. Talking back is never advisable since it only guarantees another slap.

It's May 1962, when I make my First Communion, a traditional right of passage in my family where I get to be the center of attention.

My playmate Richie is my communion partner on this day. Dressed in a navy blue tuxedo-like suit with a white bow tie, Richie looks like a bit of a dandy compared to what he wears when we're out playing, but I too am barely recognizable. I have a new white poufy communion dress with a long white veil, white socks, and white patent-leather shoes.

Mommy checks on baby Timmy sleeping in the carriage outside and shoots me daggers, a warning not to get dirty leaning against the hedges in our tiny backyard. Richie and I stand between the clothesline and the shrubs waiting for Daddy to snap our picture. Edgewater memories now get captured on Daddy's new Polaroid, which spits out color photos in 60 seconds.

It's a hot Saturday, one that's 'hotter than a cat on a hot tin roof,' an expression I heard Mommy use last summer while she waited for my brother to arrive.

The relatives are in the living room, the only place in the house with air conditioning. It's crammed with people sitting anywhere they can to stay cool, including the forbidden arms of the couch and the recliner. Most of Mommy's relatives have come to share my day, Nana and Grandpa, my two uncles -- one a priest and the other a bachelor – and my mother's older sister Aunt Kay and her husband Paul along with their two kids.

Handsome Uncle Donald, the bachelor, brings his girlfriend, Marie, to the party. Marie is very tall and very blonde. Daddy says she's a real looker, and he and Uncle Paul stare at her long legs when she's not looking. Marie is the only one not eating but drinks a highball like everyone else. Uncle Jim is the family priest, who despite the air conditioning, is sweating over his clerical collar and on his third Manhattan. Uncle Donald and Aunt Kay are my godparents and bring me a bouquet of white roses and a card with money in it.

My sister Cathleen, now in fifth grade, is the darling among the nuns and was chosen to be a guardian angel over my First Communion class, overshadowing my day just a bit. As the first grandchild in the family, Cathy is also the darling of the family.

After taking off her make-shift angel wings, she helps Mommy put the extension on the table so all the food, beverages, and Communion cake will fit. As Mommy's little helper, Cathy glides smoothly in and out between the hot kitchen and cold living room, asking relatives if they want another sandwich or high ball. Later, she will entertain the adults with her version of Debbie Reynolds and *Singin' in the Rain*.

It's a sweltering 90 degrees, and I can't wait to get out of this communion garb, put on a bathing suit, and go swimming. Uncle Donald and 'the looker' share my sentiments, and with Richie, it's down the beach we go, the one with a metal sliding pond that is so hot we have to throw water on it before going down.

———————— ⟨⊗⟩ ————————

That following February is one of the coldest months on record. Timmy is now 18 months old. I have this utter rush of love for my little brother that I don't feel for anyone else in my family. I can't explain it. It's the kind of love that is real, protective, and unconditional.

Before Mommy came home from the hospital, I showed Timmy's day-old photo to all the neighbors, hoping they would say, 'What a beautiful baby brother you have,' and most did. His round chubby cheeks remind me of a chipmunk, and sometimes I call him Alvin in the same voice as the guy in the cartoon. He smiles at this. I like to make Timmy smile. With him, I am free to be me.

Mommy doesn't have to ask me to feed, bathe, or change his dirty diapers. I do it automatically. Timmy is my very own boy doll that I get to dress in baby clothes. His new clothes come from generous neighbors and relatives who attended the baptism a month after he was born because 'God forbid a baby dies and goes to limbo.' When I'm not in school or doing homework, I play peekaboo or sing silly songs to make Timmy laugh.

When the dream of that frigid February day comes alive in my sleep, I see the jetty from a safe distance. I'm standing on the seawall shivering, looking across at my younger self on the rickety old wooden pier with its oval patches of ice scattered along the length of the jetty. It's a recurring nightmare of panic and ice water simultaneously rising over me, keeping me frozen in fear and body.

The radio says its 15 degrees outside. I'm bored. There's nothing to do after my favorite Saturday morning cartoons are over.

I remember Grandpa telling Daddy that the inside of our house is so small, you have to go outside to change your mind. Now with all five of us cooped up, bumping into each other, my eight-year-old mind understands what my grandfather means.

I have a deep need to go outside into the fresh air. There's no snow; it's just biting cold. Daddy says it's colder than a witch's titty and tells me to bundle up good. I ask if I can take Timmy for a walk in the stroller. There's some hesitancy, but both parents agree as long as I don't stay out too long.

Mommy puts a fresh cloth diaper on my brother before stuffing him into his puffy black and gray snowsuit designed to ward off cold days like this. I dress in corduroy pants, a heavy wool sweater, ski jacket and a white-knit helmet hat that covers my entire head with slits for eyes, nose, and mouth.

The arctic-like air hits the second I step outside, the kind of cold that strikes like an ice cream headache. The stroller is wide-bottomed and has little grates to put extra baby stuff on it. I wonder if my tongue will stick to the metal handlebar if I touch it. The yellow-flowered canopy protecting Timmy from the summer heat is still on the stroller. There's one strap to secure my brother in his seat, and I make sure it's tight so he won't fall out. His round cheeks turn apple red at the first touch of the cold air.

In my red rubber boots, I push the stroller in a slow trot toward the firehouse, wondering if anyone recognizes me with my face covered in the white knit hat. I look around but realize no one is out, a desolation that's rare for Edgewater.

Once I get to the firehouse, I can make a right leading to other streets, or I can turn left and go to the beach. I choose to go left, letting my curiosity get the better, anticipating what the water and sand will look and feel like outside of its warmer element.

The road to the beach is steeper than the one leading to the firehouse. The stroller glides smoothly down the hill, and the canopy flaps back into my face a few times. I defiantly push it down for a third time as we land face to face with destiny.

The tide is going out. The wet sand is dark and stiff against the lighter grainier sand. I ask myself: *Where do the little minnows hide in the winter? Does the hard shell on the horseshoe crab keep him warm, and can piss clams actually piss in this kind of cold?*

These are my thoughts pushing the stroller onto the rickety wooden jetty where the irregular slats creak with every step. There are little patches of ice that I'm careful to avoid with the stroller's wheels. I park the carriage in the middle of the jetty, where the waterline is just above my reach. Wanting to touch the water, I remove my left mitten and reach down farther than expected.

It's here many years later that time stands still, and my instinct to survive continues to haunt me with guilt when I feel myself slip into the frigid waters of the Long Island Sound, and I'm still holding onto the stroller.

The water is three feet deep, and I am only four feet high. Instantly I feel an icy, wet pain shooting up my neck. Immobilized by the bone-chilling water, I realize I'm still holding onto the stroller, which is now under the water. I try to move, but my red rubber boots grind me into the silt. My white knit-hat works against me, impeding my view, and the weight of the water inside my clothes is unbearable.

It takes every ounce of strength I have to lift the stroller out of the water. I do it for a few seconds, and as I pull it up from the murky sound, I see my brother's face panicked and frozen with fear. He's gasping for air. I scream for help, but no one is around. Timmy's eyes are wide, frightened by the betrayal. His mouth is open like he wants to cry, but nothing is coming out. His snowsuit puffs up with water, and he goes down for the second time.

Please, Dear God, please help me.

I pray, hoping to find a way to pull him out of the stroller he's strapped in. The only thing I can do is keep his tiny, frightened face above the water. My arms are outstretched in agonizing pain as I lift the stroller out of the water again. I'm not sure how long I can do this. I'm coughing up the salty water as quickly as it enters my mouth.

A wrinkly blue-veined hand comes from nowhere, and then a second, grabbing the handlebar of the stroller, pulling it up onto the pier. Standing over me is an elderly man with wisps of white hair sticking out of his fedora and a woman next to him, similar in age and hair. They seem to appear from nowhere. They both pull me up from the water onto the jetty. I start crying, and Timmy is wailing. The woman comforts me and wraps me inside her woolen coat with its soft silky lining. The man does the same for my brother, pushing the empty stroller home to meet an uncertain fate.

I'm sitting on a chair in the kitchen, just waiting with my head hung down. I'm allowed to change into dry clothes, but my hair remains wet and matted like the dog after he's given a bath. I'm shivering partly from the cold, partly from what's to come. My father is sitting directly across from me. I'm scared to look up. I'm afraid I'll start to cry.

I didn't mean to do it. I didn't do it on purpose. I wouldn't hurt Timmy. I love him. Can't you see that?

I repeat this over and over in my head, hoping that Daddy will somehow hear my thoughts and cancel whatever punishment he has planned for me.

He's waiting for Mommy to finish giving Timmy a warm bath and a bottle. She closes the door to my brother's room and stands behind my father. Her face looks angry and scary.

Daddy fidgets, rubbing the top of his lip with his finger, wavering on what to do next.

Mommy nudges his shoulder, saying, "Do it."

He hesitates at the command, and she gives him a second nudge.

The hard slap across my cheek stuns more than the icy waters of the Long Island Sound. I want to explain, say something, but nothing comes out.

My mother's glaring eyes terrify me. She looks at me like I'm evil, as though I pushed my brother into the water on purpose.

The only thing I can say in my defense is, "But --"

"But, but, but," she taunts. "But *what?*"

The forbidden tears now spill down my cheeks, mixing with the crimson heat on my freshly slapped face. No one is listening. They don't want to hear my excuses.

I'm dismissed and sent to bed at four o'clock in the afternoon without dinner or any comfort.

Daddy will not come back into my bedroom, as I had hoped, and say he was sorry for slapping me. There will be no comforting hugs or chicken noodle soup from Mommy, saying she was just frightened and upset. There will be no reconciliation for my sin.

My parents' ongoing silence toward me will only feed my guilty deed, allowing it to fester and grow inside me. Deeply humiliated and feeling without value, I cry myself to sleep, unaware of how the injustice of the day will stay with me long after the sting of that slap fades away.

TRUTH, A GAME-CHANGER

B ill comes home at 8 o'clock. The twins hear the sound of the key in the door and squeal with delight, "Daddy's home!"

They scurry out of the bedroom and rush toward him in their matching red plaid pajamas. It's an early night for their father, so I won't dampen the mood by telling him about the events of the day with my parents.

A conversation not to be had with a glib, "How was your day, babe?"

Telling the truth is a real game-changer. It certainly does set you free; and, in my case, out on my ass. I'm still trying to shake off the shock of what happened. I feel hurt and betrayed, but I'm not sure by whom or what: my parents or that inner voice in my head.

What was I thinking?

In a matter of minutes, all notions I may have had about family love and understanding got flushed down the toilet. Part of me wants to believe that once they get over the shock, they will come around. But quite frankly, after seeing my mother's vicious reaction today, I'm not so sure.

In hindsight, I shouldn't have mentioned Cathleen and my father, or even my grandfather, but there's not much I can do about it now.

And while I want to share the day's drama with my husband, I realize now I can't risk being vulnerable once again, hoping it will lead to some deeper marital intimacy between us.

I never told Bill about my father's indiscretion, but I'm sure if I said something before we were married, it might have affected the relationship he has with him today. Now I recognize too late that Bill wouldn't understand why I had to bring it up after all these years. And, I certainly can't tell him a voice told me to do it.

Like my parents, Bill believes in the Omerta, that unspoken code that says whatever happens in the family stays hidden in the family.

Back in the 70s, my husband's army sergeant father died of complications from alcoholism. Anytime the subject of my dead father-in-law gets mentioned, his only son goes into the hero-worship mode. I suspect there's much more to the story between my husband and his father, but all I get is the glossy-hero version.

Complicating matters, Bill has come to see my father as a loyal, stand-up guy; apparently, the highest form of praise between two men. In light of today's disastrous outcome, I now know better not to tell him, fearing an angry recriminating look that says: *What the fuck did you do?*

Deliberately violating the Omerta stirs up my shame, an emotion that nowadays feels like part of my DNA, something I inherited like my mother's green eyes. What happened to me at 21 was real, perhaps the only real thing I know for sure. But my parents' responses tap into my insecurities, making me feel I did something wrong. Further fueling my inner doubts, and my value, if any, I have to them.

Warmth or love wasn't something that flowed naturally from either parent. Asking for any spontaneous affection or attention was usually met with mock derision by my father.

Oh, so Joanie wants a big hug, does she?

I felt embarrassed about wanting or needing affection. My parents made it seem wrong. Like me saying shit, or any other four-letter curse word, meriting a mouth full of Ivory soap.

Mother planted the seeds for this love taboo early. She didn't want it from her daughters. She wanted *respect* and said so many times throughout my childhood. Over the years, that word would take on many subjective interpretations, leaving me confused, guilt-ridden, and stunted when seeking to find my female identity through the one woman who gave me life but didn't want to provide me with love.

As the second daughter, I avoided a lot of humiliation on that subject. I learned what *not* to do from Cathy, who paved the way for me in more ways than I gave her credit.

There were days when my sister's pre-adolescent yearning for love and validation became all-consuming. When Cathy pressured Mommy with the love question, the answer was always the same, "Of course," followed by a curt, don't-ask-me-again look. No matter how many times my sister broached the subject, my mother's terse response was always the same.

My instincts told me it was far safer being respectful and obedient than whiney about this thing called love. But no one could persuade my sister to do otherwise. I could feel Cathy's anguish every time she asked Mommy the question, and a deep flush of symbiotic shame rose in me as though I was the one doing the asking.

On one particular day, Cathy came rushing into the house in Edgewater, excited about winning an award at school. She threw her books down on the kitchen floor and wrapped her arms around Ma, who was standing in front of the sink washing dishes. I was sitting at the kitchen table doing homework, observing and listening, two traits that were quickly becoming my defining characteristics.

In playful innocence, Cathy started swinging off Ma's waist, trying to get her attention, hoping the good news of her award would prompt a different response, something along the lines of how she loved her smart daughter and was proud of her.

Instead, the scene turned foreboding when Cathy's tight grip ripped the pockets off Mommy's apron, spilling her cigarettes all over the floor. My sister's face turned ashen with fear, and goosebumps grew on my arms, wondering what was going to happen next. Would she scream at my sister, or slap her? The silence was deafening, and the only sound in the room at the time was the continuous drip from the kitchen faucet.

My mother's face stayed eerily calm as she quietly and methodically lifted each cigarette off the floor, one by one, like some adult version of pick-up sticks. After reaching for the last one, she lit it from a burner on the stove and inhaled deeply. I felt myself reflexively doing the same, and could only stare at the impression of red lipstick left on the filter. After two puffs, Ma leaned over Cathy and blew smoke in her face dramatically mimicking her pleas, "Oh love, love, love, love, love."

Looking back on that day in Edgewater, I realize nothing much had changed in my mother over the years. Getting married and giving her grandchildren hasn't softened her demeanor or her heart.

Even if there was a name for it, my mother's denial was too strong to acknowledge something was wrong in her. No spotlight was allowed to shine on her refusal to take responsibility for what she did or said, even for how she said it. No one was courageous enough to stop her from blaming others for her actions. When she was wrong, she was always right, adding to the confusion and resentment I felt by her callous behavior.

The few times Daddy tried to talk some sense into her, it backfired miserably. She would turn her prideful ego and unrelenting rage back on him, dredging up every sacred issue within their marriage, attacking his livelihood, his manhood, and any other weakness she sensed in him. My mother's visceral, street-fighter mentality, was too formidable for my father's easy-going submissive nature. Over the years, she wore him down, morphing him into a pliable co-conspirator, using him to do and say what she didn't have the guts to do herself.

The Turbulent Years

It's June 1972, the same year I graduate from an all-girl Catholic high school, and we move from Edgewater Park to City Island.

The new house is a veritable mansion compared to the bungalow in Edgewater. It has three bedrooms, two and a half baths, a finished basement, a garage, and a backyard with plenty of grass.

It's a tri-level row house, and we'll be living next to the same neighbors' Jack and Janet for the next 40 years because the local mantra is that no one *ever* moves off the Island.

Known as a boating and fishing destination, City Island juts out into the western end of the Long Island Sound, and its shape on the map looks a bit like a piece of filleted flounder.

With several excellent restaurants dotted along the main avenue to choose from, the aroma of lobster smothered in butter and garlic tempt seafood lovers to dine well into the late evening hours. In the summer, the Island never closes, and traffic gets pretty congested because the only way on and off the 1.5-mile Island is over a bridge.

Like Edgewater, everything is within walking distance. It's a self-sustaining community built to accommodate its 4000 residents, including the convenience of having a bank, post office, public school, supermarket, library, and a movie theater. Along with a Catholic church, there are several other denominations of Protestant churches, as well as a Jewish temple, reflecting the religious diversity of the people living here.

Our new home-base is rich in American history and prominence. The first to inhabit City Island were the Siwanoy Indians, who traded the Island away to an English Nobleman named Thomas Pell in 1654. In exchange for several barrels of Jamaican rum, the Siwanoy gave Pell 50,000 acres of land that included most of the Bronx, City Island and Pelham, the first town bordering the Bronx and lower Westchester County. For his role in City Island history, Thomas Pell has a street named after him.

After Pell's death, his son-in-law Benjamin Palmer took over the Island. With its proximity to New York City, the ambitious Palmer wanted to transform City Island into a seaport that could serve as New York's new commercial competition, creating shipyards and businesses that would service cargo ships before they reached Manhattan. Palmer's vision for City Island as the 'first port of call' ended when in retaliation for his treason against the Crown, British troops stormed the Island, burned down his farm, and banished him, ironically, to the very place he was trying to rival Manhattan. For his part, Palmer never had a street named after him.

Over the centuries, City Island would continue to thrive in the fishing and shipbuilding industries, building warships and minesweepers during the two world wars and luxury yachts for the wealthy during the post-war era.

My sister Cathleen doesn't move with us to City Island. She's gone. She left Edgewater last year and is now living in Texas, married to a man who owns a double-wide trailer.

Cathy's absence is palpable, and her presence lingers like a ghost. She leaves me stranded as to how to fill her role and confusion about my own.

Our new neighbors don't know about my sister, but when relatives ask, my parents say Cathy didn't want to obey the rules any longer. And that seems sufficient for their inquiry. No one in the family talks about my sister, and instinctively I know not to ask any questions. I'm supposed to imitate the same indifferent attitude about her that I see around me.

My drinking begins in high school, just the harmless experimental kind that requires a friend to steal from their parent's liquor cabinet. We drink whatever gets pilfered and mix it with orange, grape, or Sprite soda, and just enough to navigate through the emotional angst of those Catholic high school dances and that first kiss.

With Cathy gone, my family has no interest in what I do unless it causes trouble or draws attention to us as a whole. So in junior year, after failing to make JV cheerleaders, alcohol takes on the role of a part-time Paraclete, gracing me with a laid-back attitude, softening the disappointment of not making the team.

My new-found comforter also helps me forget my teen-age moodiness and ever-growing inferiority when talks at the high school lunch table turn toward plans after graduation.

While most of my friends are going off to college, or getting married to their high school sweetheart, I'm floundering in steno and typing classes in my senior year, as a just in case measure, one I had seen Cathy take.

There are no sit-down talks with my parents about what to expect after high school, talks other girls say they have with their family. Taking business classes assumes I'll go out to work as Cathy did after high school. But then what? Get married, move to Texas, and live in a double-wide?

With my ambivalence toward marriage, I'd make a terrible bride. It's 1972, and there are a lot more options for women than just being a secretary and getting married; options that require getting a college degree. My parents don't exactly inspire dreams of wedded bliss in me, either. Although she'd deny it, my mother's not happy in her marriage and remains bitter for being a stay-at-home housewife. She tells the same story about her early years in Brooklyn, over and over, and the reason she had to stop working. After a while, the monotonous narrative packs all the emotional punch of a suppressed fart.

"It's 1955, and we were living in the basement of that horrible cold-water flat in Brooklyn. Your father and I were the superintendents. On weekends, I worked like a dog scrubbing the lobby floors on my hands and knees for those people. And what do they do? Those bastards crushed out their cigarettes on the floor I just washed. The whole thing was so humiliating, but at the time it was the only job your father could get."

She pauses for effect, which doesn't work for me.

Filling in that pause, I come to his defense, "Yeah, but Ma, wasn't Daddy going to school at night for heating and air conditioning?"

"And who do you think helped him get through school? Behind every successful man, there's always a good woman."

"Wasn't he going to school on the GI Bill?"

She looks at me like I'm an idiot and continues.

"I'm young, attractive, and have this fantastic job during the week working at Book of the Month Club. They all loved me! After work, your father would meet me at the train station with the two of you. You and that sister of yours showed up looking like two dirty ragamuffins. I never knew what to expect. Cathleen usually came running toward me with some dried food dribbled down her dress and still wearing the sponge rollers in her hair from the night before."

Looking at me, she'd say, "And you? It was obvious your father couldn't tell his left from his right. Your shoes were always on the wrong foot, and your hair looked like the cats were sucking on it. I was so mortified! Everyone getting off the train just kept staring at me like I was a bad mother. How could I work anymore? Your father didn't know how to take care of his own two kids. So, what choice did I have, but quit my job and stay home with the two of you?"

Now, it's not clear whether this iconic Brooklyn tale happened the way my mother told it, whether it was a tad embellished or even a bit one-sided. What mattered was that she believed it to be true.

As she saw it, dribbled food and cat-sucking hair were the reasons her career as a clerk at Book-of-the-Month Club took a nosedive that year, permanently sealing her fate as the bitter stay-at-home wife and my father as the man without the pants.

For my Irish Catholic mother, there was no such thing as a divorce. Brooklyn became her tipping point. That pivotal moment in time when her lack of control over all the life-changes she endured in her then five-year, ill-fitting marriage to my father created a more dramatic inner shift in the way she viewed her life. If she were going to suffer the slings and arrows of living in that horrible cold-water flat without a steady paycheck, give birth to two daughters so close in age, and humiliate herself working as a superintendent's wife, then dammit-to-hell, she would at least control the one person who made that suffering unbearable.

My mother told that story so frequently over the years that I eventually grew to see it as her truth. On some subconscious level, I may have even embodied her logic as well. Many years later, I would have a tipping point of my own, spawned by an extreme set of life circumstances thrown at me and would understand the need to make someone suffer for it as she did.

I didn't want to work in an office and felt ill-prepared to do so. I hated steno and wasn't good at it. My high school teacher-nun spoke way too fast for my right brain to absorb what the left hand had to scribble, transcribe, and type in a business letter with two carbon copies.

I enjoyed reading and had a vague idea I wanted to be a writer, but that extraneous reach wasn't going anywhere with my working-class parents. And I knew it.

I cringe thinking what Daddy would say if he found out about my secret ambition. "Okay, Miss Hoity-Toity, you want to be a writer? Here, take this piece of paper and go write me up a grocery list."

Telling him I want to go to college is hard enough, but going for liberal arts is way too vague and well, way too liberal, opening me up for more parental ridicule. Not knowing what I want to study is just part of the problem.

As a veteran, my father flies the American flag outside our front door every day. His patriotism is never in dispute, but the current anti-war political climate over our involvement in Viet Nam on the evening news is a big problem.

Daddy believes that only hippies and draft dodgers go to college, those who want to take LSD to 'turn on tune in and drop out.' And don't get him started on those commie bastards who 'talk shit about this country' and run to Canada.

Tonight he's watching a certain Hollywood movie-star sit around with a bunch of soldiers talking that same shit about our country. None of this helps my argument to attend college.

I wait a few more weeks before broaching the subject. It's mid-July, and I'll need an answer soon to register at the local community college. When I get the answer, I'm neither prepared nor surprised at the response.

"Oh, Joanie, why do you want to go to college? Do you want to be one of those women libbers going around burning your bra? You can't afford to burn what little you have."

Ma overhears our conversation and looks baffled when I bring up college. "I thought you were going to study nursing in high school, dear. You look so good in a white uniform."

Perplexed, I stare at her. "You know I can't stand the sight of blood."

"Yes, I know, but you looked so good in that photo we took of you at the 1965 World's Fair in a nurse's uniform. You remember, the one where you put your head through the hole."

Four months shy of my 18ᵗʰ birthday, I spend the rest of the summer taking full advantage of my freedom from 12 years of Catholic school and the nuns.

I wander up and down City Island Avenue, exploring several of the funky antique shops and browsing the book stores learning the history of the Island. I work as a waitress, learning how to serve lobster, shrimp, and crab on big metal trays without dropping it on the floor or someone's head.

Daddy goes full nautical that summer, introducing us to the world of boating with a new Chris-Craft Seasport.

Other than taking the ferry to Hart Island, my father has no practical experience in the mechanics of navigating a small vessel. But boating is considered an essential part of this new lifestyle here on the Island, so armed with a list of must-haves: life preservers, map, flashlight, ladder, and a couple of six-packs, Daddy takes Timmy and me out on the water.

Over the next few years, Timmy will be Daddy's first mate mastering the maneuvers of the red and green safety markers. The buoys strategically designed to safely navigate boaters through the sometimes turbulent waters.

I will happily remain a passenger since I'm intimidated by the lack of yellow lines like the road and the heavy congestion plaguing the water during the boating season.

Away from the shore and on the water, I experience a different perspective. There are some spectacular summer days out on the Long Island Sound when the elements of nature converge flawlessly together in peaceful coexistence. A particular day when the sky is free from the obstruction of clouds and the wind breathes with preemptive stillness over the glaucous briny waters. A perfect moment in time when the tranquility of nature mirrors that same transfixed peace in one's soul. A divine gift to those who acknowledge His handiwork.

On one such day, Daddy and Timmy are fishing off the stern, discussing the type of bait they'll use to catch bluefish. I'm lying on the deck with eyes closed, soaking up this quintessential stillness. I feel strangely connected to the cosmos, sensing a benevolent force behind the artistry of this summer afternoon, a day created just for me. Or so I want to believe. In this state of peaceful coexistence between nature and my soul, I fancy myself a child of the universe, privy to its mysteries, contemplating a divine order whispering its secrets in my ear, telling me that all is mine for the asking.

I awaken from this mystical trance, hearing my father and brother yelling at each other over who tangled the fishing line around the rudder.

Small puffy clouds obstruct the brilliance of the sun. A breeze begins to stir, and the stillness of the water ripples from the wind. The enchantment disappears, and nature is once again at odds with itself.

I spend the remaining summer watching Daddy grill steaks and burgers on his new propane barbecue while I sunbathe for hours in a beach chair, seemingly without a care or a plan for my future.

With a brown body, sun-drenched blonde hair, and green eyes, I attract a lot of attention from the local boys who are only too happy to show me the nooks and crannies of the island. Most of the side streets have small little patches of beach where we dip our feet, smoke cigarettes, and share a bottle of beer without being seen.

There's a rickety old movie house directly across the street from where I live, showing movies that have already played in other theaters. Before it was a movie theatre, the building hosted several beauty and talent contests, a hopeful springboard for any young woman back in the 1940s and 50s who aspired to be the next Miss America.

Next to the theater is an old-fashioned ice cream parlor that stays open late, catering to the movie crowd. *Summer of '42* is playing with three shows a day.

Going to the movies becomes a popular date destination for me. If the boy is a jerk, I can run home across the street. If not, we can linger at the ice cream parlor for a while. I like to call it, 'just in case' dating.

Most of the boys I meet are *clam diggers*, a label for anyone born on the island. I learn from the locals that those of us not born on City Island are called *mussel suckers*, a dubious distinction for a female that makes me blush every time I hear it. Although I know a little bit about sex and babies, I'm embarrassed to say that at almost 18, I'm not sure how it all works together, especially with that love thing.

One of the bolder clam diggers I date passes the popcorn snickering, "Are you a mussel sucker, Joanie?"

Knowing full well what he means, I bend down to fix my sandal, hoping he doesn't see the deep blush on my cheeks coming off the two beams of light from the movie projector above. In my most impregnable tone, I manage to say, "Nope, I'm a good girl."

There will be no stopping for ice cream with him tonight.

Everything changes that September in '72 when I defy my parents and enroll in community college. They know what I did, but never bring it up. They don't ask what I'm studying, how I get to college, or how I'm paying for my tuition and books.

Hoping to get their attention, a reaction, or just an acknowledgment on their part, I make little comments here and there about how exciting my English writing class is, how I received an A on my first paper, or how missing that second bus made me late for class. For them, college isn't happening, and their deafening silence and lack of support ensures it.

After four months of going to class and working nights in a supermarket to pay for tuition and books, their denial becomes my reality. I lose heart from the pressure of their continued silence and quit school.

By January 1973, I take a full-time office job in Manhattan, marking my entrance into the real world with a sense of feeling cheated. Conversations with my parents' resume by letting me know how much money I'll contribute for room and board.

After I begin working, things in the house change radically. My mother and I were never close, even after Cathy left home, leaving us the only two females in the house. She treats me with the same chilly indifference I grew accustomed to in Edgewater. But this is different. She acts as though I'm invisible even when I'm standing right next to her. It's all very unnerving.

Dinner is usually the only time the four of us are together. And it's my little brother Timmy who brokers the silence by telling knock-knock jokes, talking about his escapades in school -- saying and doing anything to take the focus off the tension he senses, but never quite understands.

Timmy is the only one who can bend the rules. His instincts are sharp. He knows his survival depends on giving Mommy the attention and affection she inhales from him, like one of her cigarettes. With his keen sense of humor and light-hearted antics, Timmy is the only one who can balance out the skewed family dynamics, making us appear happy.

One time, he came up from the basement dressed in a gorilla suit scaring my mother half out of her wits, leaving Daddy and me in stitches and Ma with a rare smile on her face.

My mother's icy silence threatens my ability to think clearly. I ask myself repeatedly what I have done to upset her. My salary as a receptionist is $175 a week. Every paycheck, I give the $35 we agreed upon, but she continually reminds me where I could live so cheaply for that amount. Her veiled threats keep me on my toes, and I try to be extra considerate washing dishes, vacuuming, and making sure my room is neat before I leave for work. Still, her silence toward me week after week is emotionally draining. It's a brick wall that I don't know how to scale.

Perhaps, she's shunning me for wanting to go to college. I apologize to her many times for my error but get little more than a grunt response. I'm emotionally sick over her silent, cold-shouldered treatment, and become obsessed with the need to understand what I've done to make her feel this way. At 18, all I can think about is her, hoping she won't act on those threats to have me move out.

I begin seeing a therapist after work, a young Jewish guy named Jeffrey. Fresh out of Hofstra University, Jeffrey specializes in Gestalt therapy, a discipline he seems as confused about as I am. He frequently looks at his notepad that doubles as a cheat sheet and asks me questions that have nothing to do with what I'm saying.

With the clock ticking, I cut to the chase and tell him I feel unwanted, that my parents don't love me – particularly my mother.

"She's ignoring me like I don't exist, and I don't understand what I've done to make her act this way."

After bottling up these feelings for so long, the relief of saying the words out loud makes me cry, and I grab the box of tissues to blow my nose.

With a concerned frown, Jeffrey leans over and asks me if this is what I'm *really* experiencing, or is it *just* my interpretation of things.

"What?"

Stroking a beard too old for his face and wearing black horn-rimmed glasses, my young Freud explains the concept of Gestalt. He says that Gestalt works to explore the patient's thoughts, feelings, and behaviors, helping them develop a particular objective awareness on how they present themselves to the people in their environment.

"This awareness," he says, "gives the patient an ability to identify unhealthy choices and patterns of behavior impacting his or her health and well-being."

Raising an eyebrow, "So, it's my fault I'm invisible to my mother? I'm *presenting* myself all wrong to her?"

Jeffrey shrugs his shoulders and suggests we do a role-playing exercise that he calls the 'open chair' technique. I speak to the unaware me in an empty chair, and the real me sits across questioning and analyzing my ignorant self.

"I will be the intermediary," he says before I can ask his role in this whole thing.

This guy's therapeutic approach seemed too complicated for my mind to comprehend and at 30 bucks a session, way too expensive to continue playing games with myself and have him watch. I quit after a few sessions.

Looking back, I don't think my young shrink completely believed what I was telling him. After all, it was still a common belief in 1973 that all mothers loved their children unconditionally, no matter what the kid looked like, how they acted, or what they did.

His tone-deaf attitude toward my problems came from his own experience. He had two parents who cared enough to send him off to college, ones who probably encouraged that knock-off Freudian look of his.

Telling a stranger my mother didn't love me, gave me an immediate sense of relief, but the shame eventually took over, and I deeply regretted my admission to him.

With no one in my family to confide in, or offer insight into my mother's behavior and protect me against it, I was entering the real world as a shaky, insecure young woman looking for something that had eluded me up to now.

ANOTHER SANDCASTLE

Recalling my painful young adult years confirms just how inept I was at life and in winning my parent's love. After a few glasses of merlot, the panic sets in, and I want to kick myself in the ass for what I did today.

What the hell did I do? Did I think that by walking in their house and telling my father the truth, he was going to hug and kiss me? That he would admit what he did? I'm more screwed up than they are! What the hell am I supposed to do now? How will I deal with Mother after this? Oh, God, what the hell did I do?

Brian and Brendan tug on my shirt, demanding my attention, pulling me away from my anxious, slightly boozy thoughts.

"Mommy, Mommy! Daddy's going to read us a story!"

I look down into their beautiful cherub faces and smile with pride that they are mine. Their joy is contagious, and their innocence and trust overwhelming. After seven years, I continue to be amazed at the miracle of their birth and how they've changed my life.

It's this maternal shift in perspective, of wanting more for them than I ever expected for myself, that gives me the sudden courage to let the events of the day unfold the way they will. I spoke my truth. It will have to do for now.

Most nights, I'm not sure what time my husband Bill will be home. He started his own contracting business a few years ago, and taking clients out for dinner has become a frequent social ritual. Over the last year, though, he quit drinking and started attending Alcoholics Anonymous meetings. Lately, the line between sobriety and nightly socializing seems to be getting blurred.

Bill drank heavily from the beginning of our marriage. It was no secret. I assumed he had some form of post-traumatic stress from being in Viet Nam, a place he served as a sergeant and paratrooper in the Air Force. In my mind, his war experience, coupled with the financial pressure of having a second family, gave him a license to indulge.

But after eight years of marriage, his daily drinking and frequent drunk driving began taking a toll on our relationship. After a rare ultimatum by me to get sober or get out, he agreed to go to AA with a long-time friend and work associate who also became his sponsor.

Bill says the wine bottle in the refrigerator doesn't bother him. After all, wine is for sissies. And he's a rock glass, fill-it-with-rum, splash-it-with-coke, kind of guy.

He says he's not drinking, but the mints in his mouth and the avoidance of eye contact makes me suspect otherwise.

I offer to make a fresh pot of coffee to go along with a plate of chocolate chip cookies. I've read that when someone drinks, their body converts the alcohol to sugar, causing a rise in their blood sugar levels. When they stop drinking, the blood sugar levels drop too, making the body crave lots of sugar. Bill's craving for sweets has been almost gluttonous since he stopped drinking. The cookies are my way of testing his sobriety.

He agrees only to the coffee shouting out to the boys, "Get ready. I'm coming in!"

There's a frenzied shuffle coming from the children's room as they try to clear a path for their father's entrance. He announces he's going to read them the Air Force Paratrooper prayer, a military version of the Lord's Prayer.

Over the loud bang of metal trucks and puzzles getting thrown into the toy chest, I hear their tiny little voices arguing over whose bed their daddy is going to sit on to read the prayer.

I am Bill's second marriage, a May-December one, with almost 13 years difference. We met in 1973 when I began working as a receptionist in Manhattan. I was fresh out of my four-month community college stint.

At 30, Bill was the youngest vice president in DD&B, a real estate company that managed the most elite residential co-op buildings on New York's Upper East Side. In those days, he was the energetic wunderkind among his superiors and peers alike, a firm filled with stodgy, grey-haired old geezers who ruled their concrete kingdoms by barking orders behind a desk.

My husband had an outstanding reputation for being that hands-on guy, the one who had the rare combination of balls and common sense when it came to dealing with wealthy board members who often clashed with their union staff over expenses and work ethics. Rather than play politics and take the side of those who signed his paycheck, Bill walked the fine line between the blue and white collared populace earning him the esteem of being 'that tough guy in a suit.'

His well-publicized stint as an Air Force veteran, earning him a Purple Heart for bravery in the Viet Nam war, heightened his office reputation. Recognizing his service to our country, the company made allowances for his unorthodox manner, which occasionally included him wearing a black shirt with matching black tie instead of the traditional white shirt/blue tie office attire.

With his thick blond hair and cobalt blue eyes, this ruggedly attractive man stood over my desk most days, making small talk. At 18, the business world was new, and no office etiquette book covered this type of situation. Although uncomfortable with his daily presence at my desk, I remained polite.

On one particularly busy day, with several phones ringing all at once and me trying to line up the carbon paper in the IBM typewriter, he came by for his usual small talk. Stressed out, I abruptly asked what he wanted.

Without hesitation, he stared at me and said, "You."

A few months later, Bill's secretary unexpectedly quit, and I got promoted to the slot. I won't lie. Working for the office hotshot elevated my status in the eyes of others, and being the executive secretary to a vice president was heady. Bill's importance transferred to mine, and I was taking on responsibilities and meeting a whole new level of people that no steno and typing class could have prepared me.

I enjoyed the fast-paced office environment and thrived on making appointments, writing correspondence, speaking to wealthy tenants, and coordinating Bill's daily schedule. Most gratifying was seeing the approval of my job performance reflected in his eyes. I felt proud and worthy, which motivated me to work twice as hard to please him.

A few months into my promotion as his secretary, Bill took me to lunch, introducing me to the adult ritual of noon-time drinking. Over a rare steak and martini lunch, he professed his love for me and said that one day we would be married. I was speechless over his outlandish claim since he was already married and had two young children. Inwardly, I was flattered and mesmerized by this man's bold confidence and rugged charm.

An occasional lunch grew to be a weekly thing, and sometimes, he and I would meet after work. I knew it was wrong, even when the whispers in the office began, but I couldn't help myself. He was continuously paying me compliments, telling me I was the whole package in intelligence and beauty.

I found myself in the position of being that proverbial moth who didn't want to stay away from the flame.

After work, we would meet on the upper east side at some fancy restaurant. Bill usually carried a bundled roll of 50 and 100 dollar bills, always generously tipping the cab drivers and waiters on our nights out. I was becoming a real connoisseur in the liquor tasting department. One night it would be martinis, another scotch with a splash, perhaps a specialty drink like Tequila Sunrise, and always an aperitif before and a cordial after dinner.

We drank more than we ate, and most times, I was coming home drunk. I would take the last express bus to City Island, and he the last train back to Westchester. It would happen once or twice a month, and my parents started asking questions. I told them I was staying in the city to see a movie or a Broadway show with co-workers.

Bill didn't see anything immoral in what we were doing. He elevated our affair into a storybook realm, a modern-day Arthurian saga romanticizing us as an urbanized Sir Lancelot and Lady Guinevere. He was the golden knight reading his immorata poetry under a candlelit dinner, galloping down Broadway against the hot lights in a yellow checkered, ready to joust and do battle against the mundane forces to win the hand of his lady love. It was all so exhilarating for me to have the heart of one so well-rounded in imagination, intellect, and creativity, a true Renaissance man and a real-life military hero.

My sexual urges awakened around Bill. On one of our nights out, I insisted he take my virginity. It was the 70s, and despite the growing sexual freedom of women, my Catholic morals stopped short of wanting to lose my virginity to someone special.

After drinking several double martinis inside a Manhattan bar and hotel, it happened. The only visible sign of my maiden voyage out of purity was the stain on the white sheets the next morning. Realizing what I had done and had no memory of it, I ran into the bathroom to vomit.

Things changed after that. I no longer saw us through my lover's mirror. Away from him, the fairy dust cleared from my eyes, leaving only the guilt and shame. Working and dating a man 13 years my senior, pushed me out of the mainstream of women my age, thrusting me into the sordid mistress category. While I was contemplating the carnal step of having my virginity taken by a married man, young women my age were busy getting a college education and dating age-appropriate guys. I soon quit DD&B, hoping to put the fantasy of Camelot behind me.

"You're just like your sister. You need to move out." Being like my sister wasn't a good thing. My father's words cut like a knife, leaving me hurt and confused.

Cathleen, the multi-talented, rarely-spoken of first-daughter who abruptly left New York three years ago and moved to Texas to live with a guy strongly resembling my father, emerged from the shadows. I find it odd that my parents hardly talk about my sister. It's as though she doesn't exist.

They seldom call her, saying the long-distance rates are too expensive. It's Cathy who usually initiates the Sunday phone call, irritating my mother, who acts like her daughter is some pushy salesperson and wants her off the phone.

Being 'just like my sister,' a negative phrase my mother used, implied I was a bad girl, a whore, and didn't want to obey the rules. I knew it was her behind my father's threatening announcement.

Several months after my Gestalt therapy sessions with Jeffrey, my mother's behavior hadn't changed. I continued to believe it was my fault for not being able to express myself. I revisited my therapist's comments that I was coming across all wrong to her, and perhaps, it was something to reconsider.

Weeks before receiving the ominous news that I had to move out, I invited my mother to a woman's spiritual retreat. The invitation was in the desire to find a connection between us, hoping that in the company of other females struggling to communicate their feelings with each other, we could discover that bond as well.

I wanted the opportunity for us to speak, without any of the usual interference of my brother or father. I wanted to be direct and open, to talk honestly about our non-relationship. And, to my surprise, she accepted.

We arrived that Saturday morning amid a long line of females; mothers, daughters, and grandmothers, all waiting to register for the "Heart to Heart Growing Together with

God" retreat. Seeing the sheer number of women gave me hope and confidence that this was the right move. We weren't the only ones having a troubled relationship, I thought.

Thumbing through a copy of the program, I learned that after lunch, the first session would be "Life Transformation and Growth in Our Lives Through God's Word," followed by a 45-minute break. Perhaps during the break, there would be time for us to talk.

Round metal tables were set up for the cold buffet lunch, giving participants a chance to mingle and introduce themselves and find out why they came. Mommy and I sat with two other families.

The Jamison family arrived with two preteen daughters, their youthful-looking mother, and a grey-haired grandmother, all trying to cope with the sudden death of Mr. Jamison, the father, husband, and son who left a deep void in the lives of these four women.

The other was Mary Louise, a divorced single parent with daughter Darla. Judging from Darla's scowl and her mother's look of frustration, there was some hardcore rebellion going on with the daughter.

Introductions were friendly and a little awkward at first, but the two families eventually revealed why they came. They wanted to heal. I smiled and nodded in affirmation, but Ma seemed detached and uninterested in the conversation.

Grandma Jamison had been watching the two of us interact and seemed to pick up on our stilted mother-daughter connection. In a sweet, kind tone, she said, "Jesus loves you both so very much."

I nodded in agreement, but my mother just stared at the woman a little longer than was comfortable, giving her a cold hard look. "Jesus loves everybody. That's *His* job!"

I listened with half an ear to the first session of the program. My thoughts were preoccupied with the woman sitting next to me. *Who was she?* Here we were at an all-female retreat, and I got the distinct impression she didn't like being around other women. She refused to talk to anyone at the table and acted as though she was better than them. I felt mortified by her rude behavior, especially how she treated poor old grandma Jamison, who was only trying to be pleasant.

After the first session, Ma wanted to go up to the room. I agreed, thinking it might be a good time to talk. We began unpacking some of our clothes, and I brought up the Jamison incident in a joking way, saying the old lady was only trying to help us.

"She should mind her own business. I don't need her help, and I certainly don't need her telling me that Jesus loves me."

"Do you want the top drawer or the bottom one?" I asked, ignoring her comment.

"Top," and without warning, she asks, "Why have you been out so late on work nights over the last few months?"

Feeling blindsided by the suddenness of the question, I blurt out the truth about Bill and me. I told her I might be in love with him.

"You've been running around with a married man behind my back?

"Well, not anymore. We broke up. I quit the job."

She lost it and screamed at me. "Are you so goddamn hard up for a man that you have to settle for a guy who's married?"

"No, no," I said. "And please lower your voice, Ma. You asked me a question, and I'm telling you the truth."

"Your father and I raised you to have some self-respect for yourself, and this is how you repay us, by disgracing us? Miss Manhattan all grown up and going out with a married man! Oh, you're just like that sister of yours, aren't you, whoring yourself out to anyone who would have you."

Shocked by her demeaning words, this verbal tongue lashing went on for several more minutes. I couldn't defend myself. I knew what I did was wrong, and just speaking about the affair muted me silent with shame.

We never did have any sit-down, mother/daughter sex talks. Once in passing, she told me never to get into the backseat of a guy's car but didn't go into any detail.

My Catholic upbringing taught that sex was forbidden outside of marriage, and inside the sacrament, it was kept mysterious between two adults. Sex with a married man was a whole other category, disgracing the family name and considered unforgivable.

My mother and I would never finish out the weekend retreat. She wanted to go home shortly after the ill-gotten news. I feigned sickness to the retreat coordinator, and we left between sessions. The drive back home was filled with silence, guilt, and righteous indignation. I turned the radio on to funnel out the deadly mix.

In that 90 minute ride home, I realized something about the nature of my relationship with her—something I suspected but couldn't prove. The disdain in her eyes was always there. And in the manner of how she talked down to me or ignored me altogether. It was too painful for me to acknowledge, but there it was.

My mother didn't love me, but she didn't like me either. It was a truth I knew she could never admit to herself without having an acceptable reason. She found her reason that day. And I guess I found what I was looking for too. A few weeks later, on my father's orders, I moved out of the house for the first time.

RELIGION AND ALCOHOL

W e all grew up Roman Catholic in the 60s, or that's what I believed. The families in our little waterfront community in Edgewater had the same blessed objects we did. A crucifix in every bedroom, a brown scapular around the neck, and St. Christopher strategically placed on the dashboard of the family car. These were all outward signs that our belief in God and His holy saints were watching over us.

There are many ethereal role models in my religion; reminders that my life here on earth is solely to prepare me for the next. At the age of eight, I knew more about death and dead people than I did about the living and those around me.

The Church has a saint for just about every day of the calendar year, and in the day, parents were strongly encouraged to give their child a Christian name.

I am Joan, named after the French martyr, who burned at the stake for hearing voices. It's a name that will preordain my own circumstances within the family. The name Joan means *God's gracious gift*. Being born on the feast of

St. Luke the Evangelist, patron saint of artists, my puerile mind takes pleasure in having two influential saints as my spiritual benefactors.

My sister Cathleen received her name in memory of a great aunt who remained in Ireland and died in childbirth. Cathleen is the first American grandchild in the family. Her name signifies purity and innocence and is the inspiration for the 1899 William Butler Yeats' play, "The Countess Cathleen."

As the story goes, the countess sells her soul to the devil so the starving poor could eat during the potato famine in Ireland. On her deathbed, the devil comes to collect Cathleen's soul, but God in His goodness intervenes, saying that 'such a sacrificial act cannot justly lead to evil consequences.' Cathleen's name will mirror her life circumstances. She will be the sacrificial lamb, the reason for the early breakdown in the family.

Timmy is the baby and seven years younger than me. Daddy liked the name Timothy but not the Irish equivalent, Tadhg, as Mommy had suggested because there's no vowel between the h and g. My father didn't want his only son called Tad or Taddy. So my parents agreed on Timothy, but everyone calls him Timmy. His name means *God's honor.*

As a Catholic school student, I'm trained in the moral, social, and intellectual aspects of life by the nuns, our surrogate mothers in black. From first grade on, they teach us that the most critical thing in life is keeping the soul free from mortal sin, for fear of suddenly dying and going to hell.

Our young, developing minds must always be kept busy, pure, and disciplined, and any idle or 'bad' thoughts must be promptly stifled and confessed before a priest on Saturday.

Mass before school was mandatory, and fasting three hours before was required to receive Holy Communion. Any kid who stayed in the pew and didn't receive communion, we knew, was either in a state of sin or had eaten breakfast before the three hours were up. Either scenario didn't sit well with the nun who was watching.

The nuns taught us that every thought, word, and deed -- spoken and unspoken -- had moral implications affecting our relationship with God who sees all. Without understanding it at the time, my religion was grooming me and 40 other impressionable young minds toward the state of perfection-ism, a loftiness that our teachers couldn't model, nor could we attempt without feeling a profound sense of guilt and shame.

On a practical level, the nuns instructed us in everything from proper etiquette to good hygiene. Teaching us that clean hair, teeth, and fingernails, and saying 'please and thank you' was just as important as knowing our multiplication tables.

Every action, gesture, and habit got deciphered through the universal protocol of right and wrong. There was a right and wrong way of doing everything. Punishment for doing something wrong was unpredictable and could range from a surprise whack on the back of the head to being put in a dark closet until one told the truth. Whatever the punishment, or however cruel, no kid went home to tell their parents what the teacher did.

Mary was a common girl's name back then. There was Mary Jones, Mary Quinn, Mary Anne Flanagan, and Mary Louise Willis -- all who rose with me through the ranks from first to eighth grade. All these Marys were on the honor roll, even some whose middle name was Mary. I often wondered if being named after the Blessed Mother instinctively gave them intelligence, or whether the nuns, named *Sister Mary Something or Other*, favored them because of their namesake.

There was no such thing as a middle-of-the-road scholar in catholic school. We had no learning disabilities to fall back on, no excuses for lack of intelligence. You were either smart or stupid, and given the choices, it made me work harder.

The system had a loophole, though, which gave some leniency to those floundering in the academics, mostly to the kids whose mothers worked in the school cafeteria or whose fathers were ushers and sold the most raffle tickets after Sunday mass.

The let-out was character assessment, and though viewed as inferior to academics, it was no less vital to a student's growth and development. Listed on the back of the report card, an evaluation subject to the teacher's opinion could mean the difference between pride and humiliation. If one obeyed promptly, listened attentively, respected the rights of others, presented a clean and neat appearance, and attained reverence in their religious duties, it would lessen the stigmatic blow caused by any academic deficiencies.

Achieving honor roll status at St. Frances was a big deal and gave way to special privileges of being a class monitor, presiding over the cookie box, or taking notes down to the principal's office – all signs of achieving power in a world dictated by divine authority.

I worked hard for that esteemed gold-plated pin presented each quarter by the monsignor. And staying on it was a constant source of anxiety that showed in my chronic nail-biting.

Early on, my sister Cathleen set the bar high with her sterling record of academic and character achievement, impressing the same nuns who would eventually teach me. Being in her shadow, I often flailed between pride and worry, fearing the nuns' criticism of not measuring up as the younger, less talented sister.

Cathy was a popular, outgoing student driven to succeed in everything she attempted. Along with her academic and character credentials, she had a natural talent for acting, singing, and dancing, which she did performing in school plays and Irish Feis dance competitions on weekends.

My sister was the bright star in the family. Her brilliance was more dazzling than the stars on a dark summer night. And I was some dwarfed imitation revolving around her light, a diffused light that I was just as comfortable being in, as it was for her to shine.

God was mean in the sixties. He watched over little children with a ferocious eye for wrongdoing. The Baltimore Catechism described Him as omnipotent, omnipresent, and omniscient, words too tricky to say spontaneously, let alone understand what they meant. But it all came down to the same thing - power. God had it, and we didn't.

The nuns preach that God is good, but if that's true, why would He make his only Son die on the cross? They don't answer questions like that and frequently used the line, *Jesus Christ died for your sins* to control a classroom full of curious-minded kids looking for practical answers to the mysteries behind their religion.

Every classroom contained a large wooden crucifix strategically placed above the blackboard, over the teacher's desk, and next to the clock. Whenever we glanced upward toward the chalkboard or the clock, there hung the Man of Sorrows.

"Do you think Jesus thought about time when he was dying on the cross for your sins?"

"No sister," the class would chant in unison.

Along with the crucifix, a statue of the Blessed Virgin Mary adorned every classroom in St. Frances. The presence of Jesus' mother helped restore the balance of any parochial guilt we may have felt seeing her Son hanging above the blackboard.

The figure of the barefoot Virgin on a celestial cloud dressed in blue was far more pleasing to the adolescent eye than an almost-naked Jesus sprawled on a wooden cross with spikes hammered into His hands and feet. Mary's crown of illuminating stars over her head was much more captivating to watch than our Savior's crown of bloody thorns. And as Jesus' face depicted suffering and defeat, Mary's galactic blue eyes inspired serenity. She was a loving mother whose countenance seemed to say to us students: *I forgive you for causing my Son to die such a horrible death.*

In the realm of parental figures, Mary was the Donna Reed of the celestial world. She modeled all that was loving, kind, and patient in a mother. I couldn't imagine her screaming at the top of her lungs and chasing an eight-year-old Jesus around the house with a hairbrush like my mother sometimes did with me. Or, like the nuns, that she would whack the back of a boy's head with a ruler for not paying attention.

***

Three long months passed since that incident with Timmy falling into the icy waters of the Long Island Sound. My parents say I'm not allowed to take him out alone anymore, a sure sign they haven't forgotten or forgiven my misguided deed. My parents are quiet around me and don't say much. It makes me feel uncomfortable and anxious.

In that spring of 1963, my teacher announces she is raffling off statues of the Blessed Mother and St. Joseph. Sister says she will draw one 'lucky' girl and boy's name on the first day of May, the month dedicated to both saints.

I want to win that statue. I want to be that lucky girl. I know in my heart that if I win Mary, through her power, all will be okay. If Mary can forgive us for killing Jesus, then somehow, my parents can forgive me, and all will be okay.

So for the next several weeks, I become obsessed with the idea of winning that statue. But with 17 girls in the class, and several of them named Mary, I have no idea how I'll beat the competition.

Cathy and I share a bedroom and sleep in the same full-size bed. Our room is a six by eight box that includes a chest of drawers and a gray metal desk that we take turns on doing homework. The bedroom is so tiny that we can't be in it together for any length of time. A crucifix hangs over our headboard, and posters of our latest music idols decorate the other three walls. To make the room feel more spacious, Daddy painted the walls a light pink, and Mommy gave us the rose-colored chenille bedspread from her childhood and then bought new drapes to match. She says the new look will give the room some pizzazz but warns us to keep the curtains closed, even in the daytime. She doesn't want Chester, that 'degenerate' old man next door, to stare in the window when he sits on his patio drinking an afternoon beer.

The night before the raffle, I kneel at the bottom of my bed, looking up at the crucifix. Not knowing what time Cathy will be home from her study group, the plan is to pray early. With the drapes closed, I'm not even sure of the time.

I don't want to see that familiar smirk on Cathy's face if she walks in on me, and I'm on my knees. She wouldn't

understand and would laugh, bringing it to everyone's attention. My sister has confidence, and I have none and need
what the nuns call a miracle.

With rosary beads in hand, I start reciting the prayer I
learned before my first Holy Communion. *Hail Mary, full
of grace, the Lord is with thee...*moving my fingers over the
white-pearly beads one at a time as I finish each prayer. The
repetition of ten Hail Mary's rocks me into a drowsy stupor,
muddling the words in my head. My eyelids grow heavy, and
I give one last pleading look up at the crucifix before my body
slumps into a sound sleep.

The next day, seventeen pieces of folded white paper with
each girl's name gets placed in a shoebox. Sister vigorously
shakes the box, and in the spirit of impartiality, has one of
the boys pick out the winner. I nervously bite off a chunk of
skin, causing my cuticle to bleed. I hear my name and move
awkwardly through the crowded aisle of desks, ignoring the
feigned smiles on the other girls' faces. No envy could take
away my joy, believing I just experienced the miracle of
prayer. I am more confident now that the Queen of Angels
has answered my prayer and feel she will protect me against
the unknown.

My father Bill is a nice man, the consummate good
guy. The kind of guy neighbors relied on to fix their crappy
boiler or faulty air conditioner, the type of man who wouldn't

dream of taking money for his services, even though we could have used it.

With his Sears Craftsman toolbox, Daddy shows up bright and early on Saturday mornings to help neighbors build a patio or add a room to their tiny bungalow. He gives them a full days' worth of labor for the cost of a couple of deli sandwiches and a six-pack of cold beer.

My father is also a handsome man with All-American, movie-star good looks. His wavy blonde hair, cleft chin, and blue eyes mirror two of Hollywood's hottest heartthrobs, Kirk Douglas and Robert Mitchum. The local housewives call my father, *Billy the Bomb*, a nickname that makes Mommy crazy, husbands' jealous, and me incredibly proud.

As the first-born son, my dad beat the odds of repeating his father's secretly-whispered philandering lifestyle. My grandfather's name was John, a mysterious man whose birthplace always seemed in dispute. Grandpa John was a genealogical mystery; a man put together less by facts and more by conjecture. Relatives said he came from Texas, but no one could ever verify the city or town, so there's no real evidence to support this claim.

A single photo of my grandfather circulated in my father's family for years. One of him dressed in a military uniform crouching down against a barbed wire fence with what looks like a barracks in the background. My father's five other siblings have that same photo as though someone handed out copies as part of a Christmas stocking stuffer one year. The photograph is perhaps a visual confirmation of how the soldier John, stationed at the central army base in Fort Slocum, met and married my grandmother, Nora, a young Irish woman whose family lived in New Rochelle during the 1900s.

A copy of my grandfather's birth certificate I later got online, said he died in 1941 at the age of 47 from a congenital brain aneurysm. It lists my grandmother as his wife and where they lived. But the names of his birth mother and father were left blank, leaving the mystery of his roots still in question.

At the age of 13, my orphaned father inherited the legacy of 'being the man in the family,' a concept not uncommon at the time. When Cathy or I don't want to do chores around the house, Daddy loves to motivate us by telling the story of how he sold shopping bags on the corner to put food on the table, sending us both into an eye roll.

Despite his impoverished beginnings, my father is a generous man and always finds time to help neighbors and family. Over the years, he lends money to his mother and other siblings who aren't as fortunate as he to leave their South Bronx roots. Naturally, Mommy complains that Daddy's family has champagne ideas paid for with his beer pocketbook. But everyone in Daddy's family admires him and relies on his trustworthy character. He was the first and only male in his family to own two homes, buy a boat, have two cars, and provide all three of us with private school education. Although I never tell him, I also admire my father. He has that pull-yourself-up-by-the-bootstraps trait akin to his generation.

As an adult, I often wonder what more a kid could ask for in a father, one who overcame so much early adversity and went on to be a good human being? As a child, I was only looking for his love and attention, wanting his encouragement and support, acknowledging me as pretty, smart, witty, or any other adjective I could latch onto in forming my identity.

There were times in Edgewater when he asked me to ride with him to the store. At first, I was thrilled to be the only one in his company. Sitting in the passenger seat made me feel important, like a big girl, away from my sister, who was always vying for his attention. During these trips, my father rarely said a word. We would drive the whole way back and forth in deafening silence with him keeping his eyes riveted on the road and me feeling excruciatingly invisible.

The first time it happened, I chewed the inside of my mouth raw humming some non-descript tune hoping my droning would remind him that his daughter was sitting across from him. It only prompted him to turn on the radio.

Asking me to ride with him was a sign he loved me, but I often wondered why it was so difficult for him to talk to me. After all, dads are supposed to know how to speak to their daughters. Those early car rides could have been an enjoyable bonding experience creating positive memories for me. Instead, they turned into an exercise of frustration and bewilderment.

I never talked about our parents with Cathy. Despite being close in age, she and I didn't speak much. The tiny bedroom we shared wasn't conducive to sharing sisterly thoughts of any importance. Our differences seem to grow as we got older and needed more space. Because Cathy was several sizes larger than me, she and I could never share clothes. She got the new ones that took up most of our small closet, and I got the hand-me-downs from neighbors.

The gap in our physical appearance was just one of the growing wedges between us. At 13 and 11, our sibling rivalry was getting fierce, and jealousy had taken over me like mold inside a wet wall.

I secretly admired my sister's persistence to get what she wanted from the adults, whether it was convincing Mommy to stretch an already tight budget for a new sweater, or making Daddy smile by showing off her latest Irish Feis dance steps.

Around this age, I started rebelling against what I saw as Cathy's brown-nose, ass-kissing tactics to get what she wanted. The budding mutineer in me began hanging around with kids outside of Edgewater, the ones who didn't attend Catholic school and stood on the corner smoking cigarettes and cracking gum.

While Cathy was winning dance competitions, I was stealing cigarettes from my parents, learning how to blow smoke rings. I was playing the defiant black sheep pounding my chest in a tee-shirt with not enough boobs to fit a training bra, while Miss goody-two-shoes tapped danced her way into everyone's heart with a full rack of 36c's.

My father shared a kindred spirit with Cathy. He liked her outgoing, bubbly personality. It offset his dormant entertaining side, a lighthearted, amusing character that I didn't get to witness on those car trips with him alone, but emerged mostly on weekends after several hours of beer drinking.

Daddy bought a second-hand guitar in Edgewater that came with a dog-eared manual, and two used guitar picks. Several nights a week after dinner and the six o'clock news, he sat with a can of beer at the kitchen table and practiced the chords on the guitar. Darting his eyes from the manual to the fretboard adjusting his fingers against the strings, we all watched and waited for a song, perhaps a soothing version of *Kumbayah,* or any other tune, in hopeful expectation of filling our home with love and family harmony.

After a while, it became evident that my self-made father had no natural talent for the guitar; a fact my mother drove home several times by saying he played like a horse's ass. And the more she said it, the more determined he was to prove her wrong.

After a time, my father threw the manual away and found his musical niche by randomly strumming his way through a repertoire of Roger Miller tunes of *Chug-A-Lug, Dang Me,* and *King of the Road.* After several beers, my father believed he *was* Roger Miller, the lyricist, using a segue line from one song into another, "...and then we wrote."

His solo performances at the kitchen table were frequent in Edgewater. After several cans of beer, his guitar playing sprouted an alter ego, a figment of his imagination. This figment was free to play and interact with his invisible audience, telling jokes, and taking requests. The fact that my mother was asleep in the back bedroom and couldn't rip his musical efforts apart encouraged my father's doppelganger to come out of the shadows.

On one of these nights, I awaken to a harsh scraping sound against the black linoleum floor in my bedroom with what sounds like heavy breathing and sobbing. Drifting in and out of sleep, I roll back under the covers hoping to return to dreams of flying over the treetops with outstretched arms.

"No, no, please don't come in. Please stop it." My sister's voice sounds panicked, begging whatever is on the other side of the door to stop, finally catching my attention.

Something in her voice frightens me. Sitting upright, I rub my eyes, watching Cathy push the chest of drawers catty-corner against the bedroom door. It's Sunday night, and we have school the next day. It pisses me off that I have to share this cramped, boxy room with her, and now she's moving the damn furniture. All I want is my sleep. She gives the dresser one last shove, and I hear her preteen privileges of black mascara and blue eyeshadow roll off onto the floor. Then I stare frozen in horror as my Blessed Mother statue rocks back-and-forth, landing headlong next to the broken eyeshadow near the bed.

Before I could scream, I see the pale, frightened look on my sister's face. Her blonde bobbed hair is matted, and her bangs clumped with sweat. She's pressing her ear against the door. There's silence on the other side. The guitar playing has stopped, and the faint sound of a door closing to my parent's bedroom can be heard.

Shaking her head in disbelief, Cathy whispers hoarsely, "He kept calling me Mommy."

"What?"

"Daddy, he's in the kitchen. He's drunk and kept calling me Mommy, saying he loved me as he was touching me. I kept telling him I'm not Mommy. I'm Cathleen."

The dresser stays braced against the bedroom door for the rest of the night, and an exhausted, fully-clothed Cathleen falls into bed. Her back is toward me. I'm not sure if she's guarding the door, or she doesn't want to look at me. Maybe a little of both.

I pick up the unbroken statue and hold it tightly under the covers. My mind can't fully comprehend what happened, but witnessing my sister's terror and distress, I know it's not right. A numbing chill passes through me on this otherwise spring night. I'm wide awake. I look over at Cathy, who has now fallen asleep with her thumb in her mouth, a habit she gave up before entering first grade. A feeling of dread takes hold. Something has changed, but I'm not sure what.

In 1965, there were no safe outlets for emotional trauma. There was no neighbor, relative, or clergy who would listen to a child's foolish chatter about family violations. Cathleen seemed to understand that better than I because the next morning, she dressed for school and faced the day like any other, launching in herself a familiar pattern of family denial.

The following year Cathy enters Catholic high school, and there's a drastic change in her personality. My sister is moody and rebellious. She's no longer that bubbly over-achiever wanting to conquer the next teenage hurdle. She doesn't strive to get good grades or be best friends with the nuns and teachers. Cathy drops extracurricular activities like Irish dancing on weekends and fails to sign up for any after-school activities.

Instead, she takes a job at the local A&P and is attracted to older men. My honor-roll sister buys V-neck blouses revealing more of her 36C bosom and bleaches her hair light blonde. She stays out late and comes home with weird-shaped purple markings on her neck and liquor on her breath.

In just a few short years, Cathy goes from a good girl to a bad one. She flirts and fawns over guys who are practically strangers, and my mortified parents seem baffled and embarrassed by her behavior. They have many a fight over whose fault it is, blaming each other for my sister's actions. My parents didn't understand any of it, and they fought in the same kitchen that caused Cathy's transformation.

Only years later would I able to connect my sister's atypical behavior with men, and my own of asking a married man to take my virginity, with our father and the issues we had with him. But I could no more process these complex thoughts than comprehend why an inner voice prompted me to tell my father that he violated both his daughters at a time when we needed him the most.

After the crossword puzzle incident, I voluntarily moved out of my parent's house for a second time. It was a relief not to worry about being alone with my father. Paying rent on a secretary's salary was tight, and I always worried about money, and usually took on a second part-time job to pay extra expenses. I stayed locally veering off the same course Cathy had taken by moving to another state.

During my early and mid-20s, I lived with roommates and when I could afford it, alone. I took college classes at night, started writing a journal, and subscribed to Book of the Month Club reading many of the modern classics that taught me how to think and broadened my perspective on the world.

When returning to City Island for holidays and special occasions, I would receive the same lukewarm reception that Cathleen got on those Sunday long-distance phone calls. I got the distinct impression that when neighbors asked about me and why I wasn't living at home anymore, they got the same *I didn't want to obey the rules*, explanation. My pride would never let on how victimized I felt by my own family.

I often thought of Bill and how he changed my life with his love. Over time I dated several guys my age but never met anyone with his charisma and bold self-confidence, and certainly, no man professed his love for me the way Bill did.

When he called out of the blue, saying he was no longer married and still loved me, I could hardly believe my ears. At 27 and him now 40, marrying a divorced man with older children and the possibility of having children of my own, didn't seem as bad as it might have been ten years ago.

Although his divorce prevented us from marrying in the Catholic Church, Bill asked his former Air Force Chaplain to officiate the ceremony at a Methodist church in Manhattan. Three months after reuniting, we were married, and two months after that, I was pregnant with twins.

With our lives fast-forwarded into parenthood, there was no time to adjust to each other as husband and wife. I told myself it didn't matter; I knew this man, and his love for me was genuine. My happy life as a wife and mother was beginning to take shape. It was a relief to have the stability of a loving marriage and children to share in that love. I finally had a chance to live a normal, healthy life.

A FAMILY DISEASE

Scraping the dried ketchup off the boys' dinner plates, I call out to Bill that the coffee is ready. I can hear him reciting the Paratrooper Prayer to Brian and Brendan.

> Heavenly Father, hear my call; for through the sky, I will soon fall. Stand up, hook up, shuffle to the door, I pray for your will, nothing less nothing more. One thousand, two thousand, three thousand, four . . . My canopy fill 'fore I count any more. Give me courage, amid my fear, To enjoy your world's beauty from way up here.

Small pitched voices mimic and stumble over some of the more difficult words their father is reciting, which sounds more like a poem than a prayer. "My canopy fill 'fore I count any more" gets translated as, *my campy feel for I count aunty more*, creating a giant smile on my face.

Bill and I have been married for a little over eight years. During that time, his passion for all things military has evolved from a sporadic hobby into a full-time obsession. Pen and ink framed illustrations of generals, commanders, lords, and dictators, are all part of the home décor in our three-bedroom co-op apartment in New Rochelle.

Napoleon Bonaparte, Lawrence of Arabia, Julius Caesar, and Alexander the Great are some of my husband's dead heroes adorning the living room walls; coveted wall space that most married couples reserve for framed family portraits taken at Sears. Except for the kitchen and children's room, this military motif is everywhere, including our bedroom, where a stoic George Washington crossing the Delaware hangs over our headboard seemingly impervious to my need for privacy and what goes on there.

Bill enjoys sharing his knowledge of military history with anyone who shows an interest. He secretly relishes the idea that most people don't know what the hell he's talking about when he throws out British names like Lord Chelmsford and Kitchener, who fought against the South African Zulus and Boers in the late 1800s.

My military indoctrination began early in our marriage, and I watch movies like *Zulu, Zulu Dawn,* and *Breaker Morant* with the same amused expression I have watching Saturday cartoons with the boys. I chalk it up to being a good, supportive spouse to my veteran husband, who works very hard at supporting two families.

Bill introduces the children to their Scottish heritage at an early age. He enjoys telling them stories about his dead father's side of the family dating back to the 14th century. The family coat of arms hangs on their bedroom door, giving Brian and Brendan a sense of who they are.

The other side of that ancestral coin is Sicilian on his mother's side. Though she's alive and lives in Queens, he doesn't talk much about his aging mother or her ancestry. There's a familial distance between mother and son. Bill claims his mother likes his sister better than him, and that's why he speaks ill toward her. At his age, I find that explanation a bit immature. When I sometimes call him out on his casual sarcasm toward her, he tells me he never really liked women, that I was the exception. I'm not sure how to interpret that because he says this kind of crap when he's drunk. So I shut my mouth and walk away.

As to my ancestral heritage, I know very little other than I'm three-quarters, third-generation American-Irish. My mother's parents came from Ireland and settled in the Bronx. And my father's mother and her parents also came from Ireland and lived in New Rochelle as we do now. Daddy's father died a long time ago, and no one ever talks about him. Genealogy is not a topic that my parents seem interested in or wish to discuss.

For the time, I'm content listening to the stories Bill tells about his clan and how they lost the throne that fateful day in 1306, amusing us in his overstated Scottish accent declaring, "What a bloody, bloody mess it was."

Although our courting days are over, my Renaissance man still fancies himself a modern-day knight living in his own suburban Camelot. He continues to draw us into his mythical world, reading King Arthur with the passion of one who truly believes that only the purest of hearts, one like himself, can pull the magical Excalibur sword from the stone.

He takes the knight's Code of Chivalry seriously and promotes the virtues of bravery, courtesy, honor, and gallantry, as part of his own moral code of ethics.

In my Gueneverian role, I continue to play out his fantasy. I serve him fresh coffee and homemade cookies with a smile, but secretly wonder if my errant knight hasn't tarnished his armor by falling off the wagon during one of his late-night business soirees.

Tonight, I hand him a fresh cup of coffee with plenty of cream and sugar, just the way he likes it. But by the time I've kissed the twins goodnight, he's back in the den working on his latest hobby, military modeling.

The den has recently been converted from a cozy place for two, into a workshop for one. I've been forced out by the noxious smells of cement glue and airbrush paint, along with the grinding sounds of mini power tools.

Dozens of boxes of military figures in little green and gray plastic pieces, soldiers from all over the world in different historical periods, align the walls waiting for my husband to bring them to life.

Bill looks up at me with his latest man-toy, a headband magnifier tool used to see the tiny pieces of armor and weaponry so he can glue them together. His blue eyes look four times their size, and I want to smile at this amusing bug-eyed version of him, but I don't dare.

My husband's a serious man, especially when it comes to who he is and what he's done for his country, and the

Purple Heart hanging in the den is my daily reminder. He's the authority in our marriage, so it's next to impossible to gain any leverage of having a meaningful discussion with him about his sobriety. He acts like talking about his recovery isn't part of the marriage contract.

In light of him agreeing to go to Alcoholics Anonymous, I'm confused and hurt by his ever-growing remoteness. He thanks me for the cup of coffee and continues to work on his soldiers, a sign that I'm dismissed and can leave the room.

My husband is my hero, a man of substance and character, someone who rescued me from a family background of icy indifference. He's given me the love I've been looking for most of my life, the kind that is warm, affectionate, and verbal. Being told 'I love you' several times a day gives me the emotional security I need and crave, but this current cat and mouse game we're playing, wondering if he's drinking or not, threatens to shatter all I've known up to now.

As his spouse, my identity is a vague composite of biblical ideology and female television stars, a potpourri of admirable traits threaded together to create what I thought was an ideal version of me. Admittedly, I want to be that wife who is patient and understanding, a wise and virtuous woman who builds up her home, one who is a crown to her husband. But I'm not sure how that image fits in with a closed-mouth alcoholic husband who doesn't play his part in the marriage role.

I'm in a strange place mentally when it comes to Bill's drinking. No doubt, I married a younger version of my father. They share the same name and similar facial features; both are veterans, hard-working family men, and daily drinkers.

Still, I can't discuss this problem with my mother. The word 'alcoholic' has never passed her lips. And, I'm not ready to hear her righteous I-told-you-so finger-wagging, which seems to be her only answer to life's problems.

I told you he drank too much. But no, you didn't want to listen to me. I told you not to marry him, but no, you married him anyway. You made your bed. Now you lie in it!

Bill's excessive drinking came to a heated marital pitch in the summer of 1989 when he drove home drunk from his sister Karen's house on Long Island. The car ride was over an hour-long, but with dropping his mother off in Queens, it became a two-hour nightmare.

It was a hot Sunday afternoon with temperatures in the high 80's. The day started fine with Bill blowing up the kiddie pool and getting the grill ready for barbecuing. He was drinking his usual rum on the rocks with a splash of coke.

Karen is Bill's only sibling. Their widowed mother, Angela, has driven out with us for the day. It's an opportunity for her to see the grandchildren and great-grandchildren all gathered together as a family. Karen's two adult daughters are also visiting for the day. They are near my age and have children similar in age as my Brian and Brendan.

It gets a little awkward during these visits since I have more in common with my young-in-laws than I do with Karen, who is the same age as Bill's first wife.

No one brings up the fact that I 'dated' him when he was married. It's all part of the giant elephant flinging water at me from the kiddie pool in the corner of the backyard.

After a few drinks, Bill gets nostalgic and brings up his dead father, small talk as we sit outside, waiting for the steaks and burgers to cook on the grill. From the awkward tension, I get the impression another pachyderm is present, but one, thankfully, not directed at me. This one wears an army sergeant's uniform with a well-placed hand on his right hip scowling at the camera, that same intimidating scowl I've seen on my husband's face several times now. It comes from one of the only photos Bill shares with me of his late father.

"Dad was such a great, great guy, wasn't he, Mom?" Bill looks to his mother for affirmation but only gets a blank stare.

"The army turned him into a real tough guy, but on the inside, he had a great big heart of gold. He would have given the shirt off his back to anyone. Joan would have loved him. And he certainly would have loved *her*!"

I'm not sure what that last comment inferred, but there's a little eye-rolling coming from Karen, who decides it's her cue to go inside for more ice.

My 78-year-old mother-in-law sits smoking a cigarette and drinking scotch and water. Her Sicilian facial features, encased in olive skin, have no wrinkles except for the deep folds around her mouth.

I like Angela and perceive in her an inner strength, the mark of a survivor, a woman who has overcome plenty of adversity. As the daughter of Italian immigrants who spoke very little English, Angela marrying outside her culture and raising two children in an unstable alcoholic environment must have been extremely tough. But obviously, none of this gets brought up in front of me.

My mother-in-law shares only the socially acceptable pieces of her life, conversational talk about her favorite Sicilian recipes, sewing tips, and how marvelously independent she felt working in an office for 20 years.

Now sitting in an orange and green striped chaise longue, Angela takes a long drag from her cigarette and looks across at her slightly drunk, middle-aged son. Her poker-face vanishes, and a glaring *I'm-too-old-for-this-shit* scowl takes hold.

Through white pearl-rimmed glasses, Angela's green eyes flash irritation at what I can only guess is Bill's childish depiction of his long-dead father. Her reaction is something I always suspected but never said out loud.

Today, I hear a few more tidbits about the revered man, the grandfather my children will never meet, the father-in-law I'm told would have loved me, and the father who shaped the man I married. It helps to put the puzzle pieces together. In hindsight, pieces I should have put together long before our marriage.

After Bill weaves his way into the house toward the bathroom, my mother-in-law tells me in a whispered conspiratorial tone that her husband was a binge drinker, the kind who would go for weeks without a drink and then without warning, disappear for months on a binge.

"He died hitting his head in a drunken fall," Angela says impassively.

I learn that after one of these binges, it was a teenage Bill's job to drive his father to the nearest hospital to dry out. His father never sought long-term treatment. So after he detoxed, the cycle began again. Extended bouts of drinking and drying out must have caused considerable financial insecurity to the family, forcing Angela to seek employment outside the home.

No wonder she likes working in an office.

Overhearing our conversation, Karen chimes in saying her father was an angry, unpredictable man absent from many of her and her brother's school activities.

"He wasn't around much. It didn't bother me because my mom and I were usually together. We got used to his long absences, but my brother looked lost and always made excuses for him. I know he was very disappointed when my father didn't show up for one of his school events, but Billy would never say anything. To be honest, my father didn't care much about our feelings. He constantly belittled my mother and her parents for their lack of English."

From my in-laws' account, a picture of an emotionally absent and verbally abusive father was beginning to emerge, one who got fast-tracked into paternal sainthood in the mind of his only son.

And that 'shirt off his back' comment seemed like a familiar pattern in our marriage. With two families to support, money was tight, and many times my overly-generous husband gave strangers $50 or $100 because they asked.

I wouldn't mind, but there were times when we went without, so Bill could be that same 'great, great guy' he remembered from his childhood.

By the time we're ready to leave Long Island, I asked Bill several times if he was okay to drive. With two cups of coffee, he was still a little unsteady on his feet. Torn between offending him and my fear of letting him drive, I wait to see what his mother will do.

After all, he's more likely to do what his mother tells him than me.

Angela remains silent but gets in the front passenger seat holding her black rosary beads praying like it's the most normal thing in the world. Shocked, I huddled in the back between the two car seats gripping onto my children for dear life, doing my own praying, asking God to get us home in one piece.

In retrospect, the night was a culmination of all those crazy Sunday nights of riding in my father's black Pontiac, weaving over the double yellow line and reliving that old 'wing and a prayer' scenario. I promised God if He got us home safe, it would be the last ride my children and I would have to endure like that.

The next day I told Bill to seek help or find another place to live. To my surprise, he agreed. Him going to Alcoholics Anonymous was a turning point in our eight-year marriage in more ways than I could have imagined at the time.

Wanting to be supportive, I started attending Al-Anon meetings, a place where people go to discuss the problems of living with someone who abuses alcohol. In those meetings,

I learned that alcoholism is a family disease because the alcoholic's drinking affects every member of the family, not just the drinker.

I began reading several books on the topic, and the word 'dysfunctional' got brought up a lot. The term 'adult child of an alcoholic' was also an eye-opener, pointing out that family alcoholism creates certain behaviors in children that get carried into their adulthood. Reading about shame, enabling, codependency, neglect, boundary loss, loneliness, and emotional abandonment, words associated with this new alcoholic identity was like opening my high school Latin book for the first time. I had a vague understanding of the root but didn't know how it all related as a whole.

During this time of trying to be a good, supportive wife, I began wondering if I, too, was an adult child of an alcoholic because trying to figure out 'normal' became a way of life for me.

MARITAL ISOLATION

E ver since agreeing to join AA that summer of '89, Bill's deafening silence grows steadier and more intolerable with each passing month.

In recovery terms, it's a common phenomenon called 'isolating' something members of Al-Anon told me to expect. But the reality defies expectations as most nights he comes home well past the dinner hour, closes the door to the den, and isn't seen until the next morning.

Our love life is non-existent, and small talk stays within the confines of civility with him making a solicitous comment about his reheated dinner before the verbal lockdown.

If I ask if he went to an AA meeting, a red flush of seething anger comes over his face signaling my cue to back off. In his mind, any questions I have concerning his recovery is none of my business. He acts as though I'm interrogating him and have no right to be part of his recovery, one to which he continues to claim is no big deal.

While he plays commander-in-chief to his miniature militia in one room, I put together a mental laundry list of why he should consider himself lucky to have a wife like me.

At 35, I'm still regarded as attractive and would have no problem finding someone else. We have two beautiful sons to carry on his name. I don't cry, whine, or demand much from him, and despite my inner frustration, I accept the ongoing financial obligations he still has to his first family.

Justifying my value feels good because there's not much validation coming from the other side of this marital fence. I'm just not sure what to do with my growing anger and resentment.

So you can't drink anymore, it's not the end of the world! If your sobriety is no big deal, as you say, why can't you pull it together, and let's get on with our marriage? Stop whining and grieving like you lost your best friend. Goddammit, I'm supposed to be your best friend!

I tell myself I'm not the problem, but he makes me feel otherwise. He refuses to talk about this massive change in his life, in *our* life. I'm forbidden to ask anything about his recovery, AA, or what he's doing to stay sober.

Bill's mother and sister know he stopped drinking, but I can't share any of our problems with them. To discuss the details openly would be viewed as an act of betrayal because the family Omerta forbids talking to other family members about what goes on in the home.

The members of Al-Anon are supportive, but annoy me with their suggestions that I work on my own recovery.

What the hell does that mean? I'm not the alcoholic. He is!

Al-Anon uses the same 12 steps in recovery as the people in AA. They tell me to detach from my husband's disease, admit I'm powerless over alcohol and find a higher power. I think they're crazier than the so-called insanity of the disease.

―――――――୨❀Ꮜ―――――――

This idea of a higher power has been around since Bill W. and Dr. Bob founded Alcoholics Anonymous in 1935. It's the cornerstone term for today's 12-step groups, the fundamental belief that someone trying to recover from alcohol, drugs, or any other addiction, rely on a source greater than themselves. I first heard the term when I began attending Al-Anon meetings.

For me, a higher power was code for God, but nothing much had changed in the name of the Father, Son, and Holy Ghost since I was a kid.

The God I knew was still a complex concept, an obligatory guest at funerals and weddings, the one I continued to fear for not living up to His Son's sacrifice on the cross.

Jesus was the original 'half measures availed us nothing' figure when it came to following Him. Our choice was either Him or mammon, and most of us chose the latter.

Over the years, the Holy Ghost got upgraded to a Spirit. But, like a second cousin once removed, it was never heard from again.

So what was so different about a higher power? Was I missing something? If my husband found an alternative to

God, calling it a higher power, he certainly wasn't sharing it with me. He wasn't sharing anything with me.

Over the last several months, Bill's obsession with military modeling and his ever-growing detached behavior is deeply troubling. Without rum and a splash of coke in front of him, his charming take-charge personality has morphed into a reticent closed-mouthed stranger. I fear I'm losing my courageous golden knight, the man whose love for his fair-haired lady was most times reflected in his eyes. Lately, those same eyes barely look at me, and when they do, there's a shifting dishonesty in them.

Despite our marital woes, I continue to search for answers and begin to believe that his *real men don't eat quiche* philosophy is thwarting his recovery. Bill's a believer of the same book that satirized the softening '80s male culture against the rugged machismo types. He thinks that men who don't jump out of airplanes or drink hard liquor like himself are wimpy vacillating men who cling to the current social trends to define themselves.

In the past, it was fun teasing him about his GI Joe stance. Like the time I gave him a pair of pink boxer shorts with hearts on the crotch and a slice of quiche with a candle on it for his birthday. But in the gravity of our current situation, of him trying to recover from what the experts call a *dis-ease*, the inability to live in one's skin, I see this outdated he-man philosophy as a hurdle to his recovery.

Early on in our marriage, I suspected Bill suffered from some undiagnosed form of post-traumatic stress disorder and that his heavy drinking stemmed from his experiences in Viet Nam.

He often woke up drenched in sweat, screaming from nightmares, and his sporadic anger toward me and others seemed to fit the profile. I was six months pregnant swollen with the twins when this behavior began, and other than stay calm, I was in no position to do much. I wrote a letter to the Air Force chaplain who married us but didn't get a response. For the safety of myself and the children growing inside me, I learned to live with these occasional outbursts waiting for things to blow over and return to normal, which they always did.

Despite our current circumstances, I'm hopeful that Bill will beat this thing. I feel inspired by my newfound knowledge of the disease of alcoholism, and I'm confident I can help him.

If I can convince him to seek counseling, to find a professional who can relate to his wartime experiences, maybe even talk about his alcoholic military father, this might be the shot in the arm he needs to cure his inner wounds. If my husband can come to terms with his traumatic past and learn to verbalize his feelings, this could usher in a whole new life and a fresh start for him and me.

FAILURE TO COMMUNICATE

B etween the parents' silent fume over my recent visit and
my ongoing taciturn marriage, I think about the shaky,
sometimes peculiar relationship I have with all three. And
wonder if the generation gap has something to do with them
not addressing my feelings.

Like my parents, Bill comes from an era known as the
Silent Generation. Second-generation Americans who grew
up under the economic hardships brought on by the Great
Depression and World War II. They were the kids whose
parents were immigrants, survivors, and war heroes.

They had no coddling, spontaneous hugs and kisses,
no one asking them about their feelings, as most from my
generation do with our children. I can't imagine not commu-
nicating with Brian and Brendan telling them that I love
them several times a day.

All three have similar mindsets when it comes to sharing stories about their childhood – less is better. They are
masters at creating a profound disconnect between what
happened in their early years and how they live as adults.

'Let the past, stay in the past' and 'let bygones be bygones' is their mantra.

For them, memories of childhood don't exist. From what they say, or more importantly, what they don't, I get the feeling they're relieved to be out of a world where they had few options or fond memories and no control over their environment.

They don't and won't talk about it. And I wonder, without sounding like a Pollyanna, how they can erase the pain from the past by pretending it doesn't exist. Is this why they're not responding to me? Are they not capable of understanding their own feelings? I feel the harmful effects of their childhoods by how I'm treated by all three. Like wounded ghosts hiding in the shadows, I sense their presence, but can't prove their phantoms exist.

Weekly visits to my maternal grandparent's house ended in 1968 when I was 13. My grandmother suffered hardening of the arteries and needed round the clock care that only a nursing home could provide. She was 76.

That same year, despite his robust health, grandpa sold the house in the Bronx and moved into the nursing home to be with his wife. Both would live out their remaining years in an institution that turned out to be longer than either of them probably expected. My grandmother would live another ten years and grandpa two years past that.

For me, it was a silent relief to see him go. I was no longer afraid of him, worrying whether those Sunday visits were going to end up in a perverse game of hide-n-seek after him drinking too much whiskey and me cowering in a dark corner when I heard him coming. Had it not been for the nursing home, my grandfather's wound in me could have been more profound.

The secret of his abuse would stay with me until that fateful day in the kitchen in 1990 when I inadvertently blurted it out. It wouldn't have dawned on me to say anything as a kid back then. It just wasn't done. No adult, let alone a child, ever challenged my grandfather's authority or came up against the imposing six-foot-tall figure, known for his generosity in helping other Irish immigrants settle into the United States as well as being a role model for attaining the American Dream.

A more detailed portrait of my immigrant grandparents emerged years later through a series of genealogical notes researched by a relative. What I did know back then was that Grandpa was a strong-willed individual driven to succeed, and he flourished in the most adverse of circumstances.

Born in 1891, in County Cork, Ireland, my grandfather had survived and thrived in almost every conceivable cataclysm the world could throw at him at the time, including two world wars, Prohibition and the Great Depression. Soon after arriving in the United States in 1913, he was drafted into the US Army and fought in World War I. After being discharged, he met and married my grandmother in 1920. To support his growing family, grandpa drove a whiskey truck between New York and Canada during Prohibition. He started his own moonshine business in the basement of his home in the Bronx. The money made from bootlegging bought him a taxi-cab medallion allowing him the financial freedom most people didn't have during the Great Depression. Cleaning out the house before it got sold, relatives found stacks of cash tucked away in a hatbox, evidence of my grandfather's lifelong distrust in banks.

<hr>

Before her illness, I felt a sense of stability and kinship around my grandmother, whom everyone affectionately called Nana. We visited my mother's parents almost every Sunday, and the familiar aroma of roast beef, mashed potatoes, and gravy that she served on those Sunday afternoons was comforting. My grandmother's nature was quiet, kind, and patient.

One Sunday afternoon, she observed my frustration and tears over trying to memorize a poem that I would have to recite the next day in school. I was in third grade at the time. She sat with me for over an hour, helping me to remember the words.

"Read the first line. Now, reread it. Read the next line. Now say the two lines together." And this went on until all 15 stanzas were clear in my head.

Then there was the time she entrusted me with her miniature gold candelabra, a keepsake from Ireland tucked away in one of her curio cabinets. The three-prong candelabra gave authenticity to a school project of a mass altar made from a Buster Brown shoebox and green construction paper.

Memories of my grandmother are few but filled with loving fondness, so I have a hard time wondering why Mommy has so little to say about this quiet but adventurous young Irish woman who traveled across the Atlantic alone at the age of 21.

Surely my grandmother was someone who understood first-hand the dangers of traveling by passenger ship. Her older sister Brigid barely survived the sinking of the *Titanic* the year before. And doubtless, she must have felt anxious in not knowing her future, realizing she would have to rely on the mercy and kindness of strangers to survive.

Marriage to my grandfather seven years later afforded her the safety net she needed in America. But safe didn't necessarily mean freedom. As practicing Catholics, my grandparents adhered to the church's strict doctrine forbidding any form of birth control. Nana had eight pregnancies in the first 13 years of her marriage -- five children and three miscarriages. Wives in my grandmother's time weren't allowed to work, make their own money, or own a home. If my grandfather wanted to sell the house, he didn't need her permission. In a growing understanding of my grandmother's world back in the 1920s, 30s, and 40s, she was a little more of a marital possession than a marriage partner to my grandfather.

Mommy offers very little insight into her relationship with her mother. And if I provoke her, she gets testy. She's more willing to talk about her father, whom she affectionately calls Papa. Her irritability over my grandmother's inquiries melts into admiration when recalling grandpa's disciplined and controlled nature.

"Papa was an early riser. Every morning, he would get up at six. I'd get up with him and watch him shave with his Durham straight razor making sure he didn't cut himself. He would have his tea with a bowl of prunes and read the newspaper before taking the taxicab into Manhattan. After dinner, he would always walk for an hour to get his exercise. When my father made up his mind to do something, like giving up cigarettes, 'he did it just like that,' she said, snapping her fingers."

It was during one of these rare conversations with my mother that I learned grandpa introduced her to cigarettes and took her to the local pub for her first drink of whiskey and soda. I find that custom if it was such, bizarre and a bit creepy thinking of my father doing such a thing. But in my mother's time, it was considered a father's duty to keep his daughter's virtue intact, and going into a bar by herself or with other women was deemed inappropriate.

IMBROGLIO

There's an ominous cloud lingering over the family. No one is talking. Even though I live in the same apartment complex as my brother Timmy, I haven't seen or spoken to him in a couple of months. And while I told Cathy ahead of time I was going to confront our father, I haven't heard from her either. She's probably mad at me for telling them about grandpa. I'm sure Ma called her right after and accused her of being a liar too, keeping Cathy silent with shame.

With all this unsettling drama, I try to keep busy. Two nights a week, I take college classes, and during the day, I work as a counselor where the boys go to summer camp. School and work give me a sense of moving forward with my life, but I can't seem to shake off the intense anxiety over my marriage.

With Bill still isolating and me continuously frustrated, he and I are at an impasse. Convinced I need to do and act on something, I finally research therapists who served in Viet Nam, professionals who I feel can relate to Bill's PTSD and excessive drinking. I'm sure if he got in front of one of these guys, he would be able to tell him things he can't say to me.

After spending a couple of hours in the library, I find several names in the New York area who seem qualified to help him. I feel hopeful my efforts will be appreciated and that all he needs is a little push forward in the right direction.

It's a Friday night when I approach Bill. He's in the den working on his soldiers when I hand him a neatly, type-written list of therapists with addresses and phone numbers, explaining to him why I thought he needed to see a professional.

He stares silently at the list for a long, long time. *Maybe he recognizes the names of some of these guys from the service.* So I nervously keep talking, hoping he understands my intent is only to help. When he finally does look up, his hands are shaking, and the contemptuous sneer on his lips takes me aback. He throws the paper down at my feet as though I just handed him a divorce decree and goes back to what he was doing. Dumbfounded by this inappropriate response, I leave the room without saying another word.

The following day we drive out to Karen's house for another barbecue. Bill's mother isn't with us, and except for the chattering of the boys in the back seat, the ride to Long Island is uncomfortably silent. I feel hurt and misunderstood by his negative response about going into therapy.

I bruised his ego, what's the big deal? It's only therapy. Why is he so mad? The people in Al-Anon talk extensively about how the family dynamics need to change to survive. I'm only trying to offer him an alternative.

If he wasn't willing to open up and talk about his feelings, I don't think I could survive the silence between us much longer.

Bill is outside in the backyard stoking the coals for today's barbecue. Karen and I are in the kitchen. I'm peeling the green rind off a second cucumber for the salad, and she's taking the marinated meat out of the refrigerator. She comments about how everything is almost ready.

On my second glass of merlot, I get the courage to talk to my sister-in-law, wanting to share my concerns over her brother's sobriety and the connection with his war experiences. I know I'm risking Bill's wrath if he finds out I'm talking to her, so I take a few more sips of wine for added courage.

"You know, Karen, if your brother got the professional help I think he needs, I'm positive he could get sober a lot quicker. I just know and feel in my heart that many of his emotional problems stem from his time in the Air Force and fighting over in Viet Nam."

There was a long silence, longer than expected, and I turned to see if she heard me.

With a perplexed look on her face, Karen stands motionless, holding the pan of marinated meat.

"What?" I ask, shaking my head.

"Joan, my brother, was never in the Air Force, and he certainly *never* served in Viet Nam. Is that what he told you?"

She started to laugh but then caught herself.

"The truth is he only did a year of ROTC in college."

A Spiritual Rebirth

Timmy walks down the blacktop driveway of our apartment complex, heading toward his car. He's looking downward, jingling his keys. I'm returning from the supermarket, carrying a bag of groceries from the station wagon. We are two ships in the night.

He looks up. I give him a big smile. There's a surprised look on his face, but one that says it's not a pleasant surprise. I now realize my not seeing him over the last few months is by design.

"Hey, how are you?" I ask.

The look on his face reads, *don't bring it up*, but I do.

"I guess you know what happened."

"Yeah, ma called me right after it happened. She said she kicked you out of the house. She wanted to know if I knew anything about it. I told her, absolutely not!"

"I didn't want you to know. I didn't want to put you in the middle of all this."

"Well, I am, and you did." His angry words take me by surprise.

Timmy looks distracted. A part of me hopes he'll ask if it's true; if daddy and grandpa could do such a thing. But looking at him now, it's clear he doesn't want to know the truth. There's a long silence between brother and sister. His pale blue eyes are defensive and seem to say: *I don't understand why you did such a stupid fucking thing, but I want no part of it.*

Finally, he shakes his head and throws his hands up in mock helplessness, saying he's late for work. His sharp dismissive tone tells me he's chosen a side, and it's not mine. Hearing the sound of his muffled engine roar down the street, I realize this is the severing of my last blood tie here in New York.

Standing alone, I feel the dizzying aftershock from this latest act of betrayal.

How much can a person take?

Karen's words, *he was never in the Air Force, and he certainly never served in Viet Nam,* make my head throb. Reliving this marital bombshell over and over feels like an earthquake under my feet. I haven't been able to grasp the magnitude of Bill's lies and deceit. It's incomprehensible to fathom how someone can fabricate a story like that and keep it going for such a long time. And now that I know, he's completely shut down, leaving me in a deeper silent hell.

Being shunned by my brother now feels like the ground is going to swallow me up. I stagger backward from the emotional weight of its impact. The grocery bag slips from my arms. I clutch my chest, hoping to ward off what feels like a dozen sharp knives rapidly thrusting into my heart. I can't breathe.

Is this a heart attack? Am I about to die? Is this what death feels like? Please do it and get it over!

Standing alone in the middle of the parking lot, drowning and begging to die, a mini-squall of wind comes from nowhere. This sudden rush of wind disturbs nothing in my surroundings, not the leaves on the ground or the bag of groceries inches from my feet. This wind is swirling around me, like a warm bath of love filling me with what I can only describe as ecstasy. It's blowing around me without so much as a strand of hair moving on my head.

I'm not afraid. I feel its benevolence. I close my eyes and let out a deep sigh feeling this miraculous act of nature engulf me, hoping the rapture will last. At that thought, the wind ceases. In seconds, it's over.

My eyes gaze upward toward the sky. I somehow know that the old *me* has left my body like some ghostly apparition. It's a transcendental experience, the one we have when our time here on earth ends. I'm unable to see the old me, but instinctively I know she's gone, disappearing somewhere into that blue hue of sky and clouds. I whisper, *goodbye,* waving to my old self like some childhood friend embarking on a journey, one that I will never see again.

In the ebb and flow of a breeze, I have been transformed, cleansed in a new body and mind, a new me — a spiritual gift no Saturday confession could ever achieve.

The prospect of death is gone. God is real and has been watching over me all this time. I'm not alone. I have been reborn.

THE EULOGY

G od's sanctifying grace was undoubtedly present and holding me together that chilly March morning, when neighbors, friends, and family gathered outside St. Mary's church to attend my father's funeral.

At the age of 63, my father was dead. He took a nap one Sunday afternoon and never woke up. His death was sudden and without warning. The coroner ruled it a heart attack.

High pitched vocals from the organist, preparing for her rendition of *Amazing Grace*, filled the silence of the church.

"What a peaceful way to go," many of the neighbors whispered.

Under different circumstances, I would have agreed. But, in the aftermath of having no closure and my mother's latest accusation that my father died from a broken heart caused by my lies, I felt more like an aberration than a daughter in mourning.

My grieving widow of a mother looked stoically chic dressed in a black and white wool dress and a matching veiled pillbox hat that covered her eyes. She sat in the front pew, clutching my brother's arm for emotional support. Timmy looked visibly shaken and sad.

Presiding over the funeral mass was my mother's brother, the priest, the one who spent many a night at our house sleeping off too many Manhattan cocktails and often told bawdy stories about his travels outside the rectory. My uncle had the honor of giving the eulogy as well.

What a hard-working husband and father Bill was to his wife and family, and as his brother-in-law, he would treasure all the barbecues, good times and laughs they shared.

My uncle said he would always be grateful for having a home base, a place to stay whenever he was in town, and that my father was like a brother to him.

In a pastoral tone worthy of any Sunday sermon, my misty-eyed uncle glanced down at his 'favorite' sister from the pulpit telling his audience how much my mother would miss her loyal, loving husband of 42 years. Theirs was a true storybook romance of youth into maturity built on love, admiration and mutual respect for their roles as husband and wife. He was the love of her life, and she adored him to the end.

With widespread arms, he acknowledged the neighbors and friends scattered throughout the church thanking them for coming and praising my father's reputation for being a good Samaritan to those on the block who needed his mechanical skills.

He spoke of Timmy with warmth and affection, in glowing terms of how close father and son were in sharing their love of boating, fishing, and cars. How my father's influence in his field got my brother into that same career of heating and air conditioning, using the fulsome phrase 'like father, like son' as his commendation on their relationship.

After a long pause and a deeply extended sigh, my uncle turned his attention to Cathleen and me huddled next to each other, sitting directly behind our brother and mother.

Neither one of us knew what to expect. Although I hadn't seen my sister in years, our lasting bond was that memory of me witnessing Cathy push the chest of drawers against the door in Edgewater. We spent the morning reminiscing and laughing at all the silly things my father would say and do in those earlier years when we were kids.

My own life was in tatters. Bill and I were in the middle of a divorce, and my future was uncertain. The one thing I had to hold onto was this incredible grace living inside me, giving me hope that God was watching over me and could get me through this exceptionally stressful time.

Looking directly at Cathy and me, my uncle's facial expression took on the frown of a monsignor who wasn't pleased with his pupils on report card day. He praised my father for his years of hard work and sacrifice that enabled his only two daughters to have such an exceptional Catholic school education in a time when my parents could ill afford it.

Period. End of story.

There it was. From the brief and cryptic comment came the subliminal message. It was apparent my mother told my uncle what I did. And, in turn, he was letting Cathy and I know in front of God and the whole congregation that good

Catholic girls don't disrespect their parents and grand-elders by telling lies about them.

So, in the final moments of grieving our deeply flawed but much-loved father, my priest of an uncle talked about his two nieces like we were an obligatory afterthought. In the annals of my father's life here on earth, Cathy and I had just become ecclesiastically humiliated and relegated to a post-it note in one of the most pivotal relationships either one of us would ever have.

"When my father and mother forsake me, the Lord will take me up."

PSALM 27:10

Into the Wilderness

Three days after signing the final divorce papers, the boys and I left New York and found ourselves in Texas. Upon arriving in Houston that July 1992, I felt like some proverbial fish out of water with two little guppies trying to make sense of how we wound up in this glass bowl of heat and humidity.

Cathy met us at the gate with all the joy and exuberance she reserved for arriving guests. The fact that the three of us weren't visiting, but were now going to live in the Lone Star State, slowly began to sink in.

Overnight, I had gone from being married to divorced, home to homeless, and now my status as a boarder in my sister's house created tears in my eyes. I was ill-prepared for the repercussions of what death and denial had created, destroying everything I knew and landing me headlong into this blistering hubris state threatening me with a "Don't Mess with Texas" sign.

I often cried, silently and alone, so that the twins, now nine years old, wouldn't know my real feelings. I took long showers in the hard Texas water, relieving my pent-up tears.

I wanted to function as an upbeat, happy mother pretending to the two most important people in my life that everything would remain the same, and the impact of mommy and daddy's divorce wouldn't shatter their lives.

I questioned God's wisdom of leading me into this god-forsaken hell hole. And kept asking myself, how did I get here?

Not by choice, that's for damn sure.

The lack of control over my own life was deeply unsettling. I held onto the idea of staying in New York long after it was apparent I could no longer afford to. After his exposure that he wasn't in the military, Bill moved out and rented an apartment. His adamant refusal to discuss or even acknowledge how his deception and lies ruined our marriage was infuriating. He wanted everything to stay the same, a demand impossible for me to accept.

I thought he drank alcoholically because of his war experience. Now realizing he wasn't in Viet Nam or even in the Air Force, as he claimed over the last 20 years, I didn't know who the hell he was. And who was this chaplain guy who married us? Were we actually married? Where did he get that Purple Heart? How did he know so much about military history? Who was Bill? This last question terrified and repulsed me at the same time.

Our brief stint at marriage counseling was useless since he somehow conned the therapist into believing we were only going through a marital rough patch.

He manipulated our children and finances as leverage to get back together. He wanted our marriage to stay the way it was without answering the question I asked him most often. Why?

My pleading went on for months, and then I finally got the answer I so desperately wanted but found too difficult to hear.

Spewing his hateful, pent up anger toward me, my erstwhile knight let me know exactly how he felt.

"So fucking what? What's the big fuckin' deal about what I did? And what are *you* going to do about it? You can't do a damn thing."

And that's how I arrived in Houston.

I didn't see this pot-boiling city as a new opportunity to start over, but rather as punishment from the very God who revealed Himself to me not too long ago.

Ironically, outside of my failed marriage and strained family relations, my own life in New Rochelle was starting to take shape. I went from a volunteer to a paid pre-k school teacher during the week. And on Sunday, I taught catechism class to second graders. My dean's list status through college night classes got me a state teaching scholarship. I was becoming a relevant person in the community. But it all got destroyed in the financial aftermath of the divorce.

Now starting over, just three months shy of my 38th birthday, I felt lost, alone, and disoriented. I had been dropped down into another land like some modern-day Wizard of Oz character who kept wondering how she got here.

My sister lived in a small suburban town located south of Houston. Quaker Meadow had a 1960s retro feel to it. Despite my initial impression of Texas, her hometown resembled a Norman Rockwell painting where God, family, and community, with its corresponding values, seemed very much alive. Quaker Meadow was a comforting reminder of a more innocent time back in Edgewater Park when the spirited child in me believed all was good in the world.

One of the first things I noticed was the congeniality of the people. Strangers smiled and made eye contact wherever I went; only I went around acting like some frenetic New Yorker rushing toward her destination.

It boggled my mind when a driver slowed down for a yellow light, instead of stepping on the gas. Jerks like that up north always got a blast of the horn from everyone behind him.

Cashiers at the local supermarket were pleasant and talked to me as they rang up and bagged my food. They even took the groceries out to the car, refusing a tip.

In Quaker Meadow, there were no high-rise apartment buildings, ghettos, or billowing smokestacks blocking the view of the Texas spacious skies. Most homes were expansively set apart from each other, and no one lived close enough to peep inside their neighbor's window, as I remembered in Edgewater.

The town had no public transportation. There were no buses or trains, no gypsy, yellow, or checkered cabs. And to my surprise, there were no cowboys on horses galloping down Quaker Meadow Drive.

On the contrary, Quaker Meadow Drive was a modern tree-lined main street permanently decorated with Texas and American flags. We arrived in Houston that Friday before the annual Fourth of July parade, a magnificent display of red, white and blue floats, banners, smiling faces, happy children, barking dogs, loud music, colorful fireworks, and the tangy smell of barbecue. This All-American apple pie oasis would be our new home for the next several years.

School life began in August, a month before it did in New York. It was a mixed blessing because the boys didn't have too much time to dwell on their new surroundings. All three of us were sleeping in one bedroom at my sister's house. I registered them at the elementary school and enrolled myself in the local college to finish the degree I started up north.

Cathy gave me her spare vehicle, a red Plymouth Voyager with just under 90,000 miles on it. With no mass transportation available, I was grateful for any means to get around. My suburban surroundings in Quaker Meadow turned more rural driving toward the college, and the passing scenes of hay, cattle, and horses became more prominent.

My father's ignorant phrase, 'shit kickers' came to mind, and I had to laugh because now, I guess, I was one of those kickers. Before he died, there were no words of reconciliation between us. No comfort, no concern, no sorry, or please forgive me on his part. It was only by chance that I ran into him six months before he passed.

My father was buying a carton of cigarettes from a storefront that doubled as a barbershop in the back. After the twins were old enough, my father took Brian and Brendan to this same place to get their first haircut. It then became a tradition to bring the boys there for their regular cuts.

My heart skipped a beat when I saw him walk through the door. A mixture of excitement and apprehension filled my heart. He was alone. I was sitting across from the row of barber chairs reading a magazine when I looked up and saw him from the corner of my eye. He saw me in the mirror, but I didn't wait to see what he would do. I stood up and went to him.

"Hi, Daddy," was all I could say. I kissed him on his cheek.

He looked over at my sons, who were frantically waving at him from their chair.

"Are you getting your haircut, too, Poppy?"

My father gave them each a big hug, assessing the barber's work with a paternal nod. The scene seemed so reminiscent of that first time.

If my father's original plan was to get a haircut that day, he changed his mind. With a carton of cigarettes under his arm, we stood by the doorway for what seemed an eternity.

And, finally, with tears welling up, I said, "I miss you. And I love you, Daddy."

He looked down at the floor and, with a weary sigh, said, "Yeah, but you don't love your mother."

He turned and walked away.

Dumbstruck by his words, I stood in the storefront doorway, feeling insignificant, ashamed, and all alone. My father never once mentioned that day in the kitchen. Months later, he would go upstairs for a Sunday nap and die of a coronary.

I saw his last damning words as a testament to my relationship with him. If I couldn't love my mother, how could he possibly love me as his daughter? The implication of his words felt like a fresh punch in the stomach, making me hate myself all over again for bringing up the molestation in the first place.

WE'RE NOT IN KANSAS
ANYMORE, BOYS

E ighteen months after arriving in Texas, I graduated with
a degree in English literature and now needed to find
a full-time job. I picked up the *Weekly Gazette,* a free newspaper on the rack outside a supermarket, and scanned the
classifieds.

With the help of my sister, a part-time job at the college,
and Bill's sporadic child support checks, the boys and
I moved out of Cathy's house. We were now living in a
two-bedroom apartment in the middle of town.

Here in the south, apartment-living is considered temporary, and most complexes only offer short-term leases. In
upper-middle-class Quaker Meadow, renting is a lifestyle
reserved for the less fortunate or those with single-parent
status. To my chagrin, I fit both categories, but quite frankly
was in no position to challenge the stigma. I had to accept
my new station in life and was grateful that the boys and I
no longer had to share one room.

Our two-bedroom duplex had two bathrooms, a patio, central air conditioning, and a community swimming pool. I asked the apartment manager if there was anything longer than a six-month lease since I wanted to lock in the $500 a month rent for two years, and was bluntly told, "This is not New Yawk."

My job prospects seem limited to the immediate area, so I could be nearby if the boys got sick or dismissed early from school. The boys were thriving in their southern environment with new friends and the extracurricular activities of football, baseball, and basketball, to keep them busy. I didn't want to upset their daily routine and after-school activities by trying to find a job inside Houston's inner loop, which without traffic, could be an hour's commute home.

Disheartened by the scant classifieds that didn't fit my limited work experience, I thumbed through the rest of the newspaper. The weekly editorial caught my eye. The editor of the *Weekly Gazette* wrote a piece on gun control and the need for it here in the great State of Texas, or more specifically, here in Quaker Meadow. I couldn't believe my luck, or my eyes, as I read the author's unconvincing argument against the right to bear arms because of the negative lesson it was teaching children. As a transplanted Yankee, I knew that guns in the south were as sacred as their Friday night football games.

What was this person thinking? Surely, she's not going to last long as the editor.

And as predicted, bombarded by hundreds of protest letters from local NRA supporters, the newspaper was forced to print a retraction and decided it was time to look for a new editor. When I saw the ad for a reporter/editor, I jumped at the chance to apply.

My background in writing was limited to term papers and personal journaling, but the owners of the newspaper, Tracy and Chip Lauder, a husband and wife team, liked the fact that I was from up north. Originally from Chicago, Chip referred to New York as a sister state and mentioned being an avid Ranger's hockey fan, heightening my chances of getting the job.

Having this simpatico relationship with people from the south wasn't always the case. My Texas History teacher, who was actually from Louisiana, wouldn't give me an A if I got on top of the desk and whistled Dixie with two spoons on a knee.

As soon as he heard my Bronx accent during an oral presentation, his whole demeanor changed. After giving me a B minus for the class, his smirking, hat-tipping gesture toward me on the last day let me know the war between the states was still very much alive in this bayou ballbuster's mind.

On the whole, though, being from New York gave me an edge. The perception with the locals, however true or false, was that New Yorkers were quicker, savvier, and more efficient. Not wanting to disappoint, I went with that impression during my interview with Tracy and Chip, hoping to land the job.

For several years, Tracy Lauder was the saleswoman for the *Weekly Gazette* selling advertising space to the locals before buying the newspaper from the previous owner, who retired somewhere in Missouri. She purchased the family-owned paper just six months before I came along.

Lauder said her mistake with the former editor was all part of her trial and error period as the new publisher. Despite my lack of journalism experience, Tracy liked the fact that I had some 'snap' as she called it and hired me on a trial basis.

In truth, the *Weekly Gazette* was considered a second-rate newspaper compared to its local competitor, a corporately-owned deep-pocketed publication known as the *Herald-Times*. Both papers published for Quaker Meadow and a town called Apple Butter, and both came out on Wednesday.

Along with a non-existent readership, the *Weekly Gazette* had an abysmal reputation for being known as the 'ditch paper' primarily for its inferior quality both in the caliber of journalism and production.

At the time, the Gazette was a free newspaper thrown in people's backyards on Wednesday. The substandard quality included the black ink that smudged on the unsuspecting reader's hand when they picked it up, creating the standing joke that when the *Weekly Gazette* got thrown in your yard, it got thrown right back.

As the newspaper's only reporter, photographer, and typist, I would be covering weekly city council and monthly school board meetings, police activities, ribbon cuttings, and anything else newsworthy for the good people of Quaker Meadow and Apple Butter.

It was a shoe-string operation with the promise of future editorship. And, it came with the excitement of knowing the only direction we could go was up!

A few weeks into my new journalism career, the office gets a call. There's a hostage situation taking place at one of the apartment complexes in town, and a 37-year old white male is holding a woman and two children at gunpoint.

With no other information, Chip tells me to grab the camera and a notepad, and we jump into his pickup arriving on the scene in time to see a half dozen police officers pile out of a truck and storm the apartment complex.

These highly-trained officers have the word CART white-lettered on their black vests. It's an acronym I'm told stands for *Combined Area Response Team,* a southern variation of SWAT.

Standing behind the designated yellow-taped crime scene area, Chip introduces me to Chase Tyler, Quaker Meadow's police chief. As a former journalist, turned police officer and now the chief of police, Tyler and I have an instant connection.

He gives me a wink saying he too was once a cub reporter and can appreciate getting a scoop ahead of the competition. Being viewed as a 'cub' on the verge of turning 40 makes me want to hurl, but it's evident that the late 50ish chief is well-intentioned and aware of the newspaper's underdog position in the community. So, I go with it, and with pen and pad in hand, the chief fills me in on what he knows.

The man in question is the estranged husband of the alleged intended victim, who recently moved to Quaker Meadow to get away from him. They have two young daughters, a three-year-old and an eight-month-old infant. On the wife's way to work that morning, the estranged husband confronts her in the parking lot, carrying a loaded semiautomatic pistol.

That's an excellent way to woo her back.

Tyler said the wife managed to escape to a neighbor's apartment and made the second of three 9-1-1 calls recorded that day. The initial phone call was made by someone who saw the couple fighting in the parking lot.

The third and final call came from the wife's mother, who was babysitting the two children. She frantically told the 9-1-1 operator that her son-in-law fired a shot into the apartment door and was now inside waving a gun at her.

By the time Chip and I arrived on the scene, the emergency response team was filtering into the apartment building with sniper rifles pointing in the same direction. From where I'm standing, it's difficult to see where one marksman starts and another begins. They look like one long black line.

I find it all a bit surreal and expect a camera crew from *America's Most Wanted* to come popping out of a bush at any moment. Despite southern perceptions, nothing in my New York experience has prepared me for anything like this.

The chief nervously puffs on another cigarette, waiting for word on his walkie-talkie. While Chip and I stand by, I get tempted to ask my new compadre for a cigarette. But in the seriousness of the whole situation, I refrain from any presumed familiarity to maintain a professional image.

Several minutes later, the CART team emerges from the building, shaking their heads, looking defeated from the outcome.

An ambulance crew places the adult female onto a gurney rushing her off to the nearest hospital. A Coroner's van arrives a few minutes later, and two little black bags and one adult bag come wheeling out of the building. The mother of the lost children falls on her knees, shrieking in horror.

The minutes leading up to the murder-suicide deaths of three-year-old Brooke, eight-month-old Callie, and their estranged father got recorded in that final 9-1-1 call made by the mother-in-law. The tapes were released to the media two days later. At the police station, Chip, Tracy, and I hear a cacophony of gut-wrenching pleading and wailing until the sounds of five .38-caliber gunshots have the last word.

His name was Adams, and he shot his two baby daughters once in the head. He then turned the gun on his mother-in-law, who survived gunshot wounds to the neck and shoulder before deliberately using the last bullet to shoot himself in the head.

We drove back to the office in silence, all three of us reliving the sound of those murderous bullets and screaming innocent children in our heads. I started to cry.

The Lauders' have been residents of Quaker Meadow for the last ten years. Chip feels the need to apologize, saying nothing like this has ever happened before and feels confident it won't again. Tracy agrees, adding that the family only moved to Quaker Meadow to get away from that maniac husband and weren't actual residents. Their faith that this is a one-time tragic occurrence is semi-comforting.

Still shaken, I take the rest of the day off and feel the need to pick up Brian and Brendan early from school. Opening the side door to the van, I cover them with hugs and kisses saying, "We're not in Kansas anymore, boys!"

Ignoring the puzzled look on their faces, I surprise them with an unexpected trip to the local TCBY for ice cream.

THE HATFIELDS
AND MCCOYS

The cities of Quaker Meadow and Apple Butter lie north of Houston and south of Galveston. Geographically snuggled up against each other, but located in different counties, the makeup of these two towns was surprisingly diverse with shades of the old Hatfield and McCoy feud still alive in how they viewed each other as neighbors.

Located in Galveston County, Quaker Meadow was founded in the late 1800s by a conservative religious group whose value on God, family, and education continued to thrive when I arrived there in 1992. At that time, the city covered approximately 21 square miles and had a population of about 29,000.

Economically, the town grew faster and had a more diverse populace than Apple Butter, primarily from the opening of the NASA Space Center in the 1960s and the growing number of oil and gas companies that popped up across Houston in the 70s and 80s.

Transplants from all over the country, highly educated, well-paid engineers, scientists, and executives relocated their families to Quaker Meadow because of its convenience to downtown Houston, its reputation for an excellent school system, and a marketed suburban feel.

Founded by a Polish nobleman in the 1800s, Apple Butter got its name from the soil's ability to produce hundreds of acres of apple, fig, and pear orchards inside just as many dairy farms.

Located in Brazoria County and twice the size of its Hatfield counterpart, Apple Butter's population of 38,000 was more spread out and less developed, with one-lane Farm to Market dirt roads connecting neighbors.

Considered a hodgepodge farming community, Apple Butter might have stayed in the country bumpkin category, had it not been for the ambition of one man. An enterprising city manager who had the unique ability to transform a sow's ear into a silk purse, eventually giving Quaker Meadow a run for its money.

More often than not, it was the wrath of mother nature that brought these two towns together, creating in them a sympathetic bond despite their apparent differences. Flash flooding was frequent in both cities, and sudden torrential downpours, causing flash floods, were very much a part of the southern climate. This kind of rain could be far more damaging than blizzards in the Northeast.

Both towns experienced flooding that submerged whole subdivisions for weeks at a time. The rain contradicted the government's 100-year flood plain plan that claimed this type of flooding would occur only one percent of the time in a century. Yet, the razing of flood-prone neighborhoods happened quite often. And it was my job to report how the two cities coped with such devastation and their on-going battles against the local drainage districts whose job it was to prevent such things from happening.

Easing into my new journalistic career as the voice for the *Weekly Gazette*, I had a marvelous sense of God's hand on my shoulder, guiding me into a world that would test my intellectual and writing muscles to its limit.

There was little time to learn the sometimes confusing municipal language used at city council meetings and then translate it into an understandable format for the reader. I worked long, hard hours, and it seemed like I was always on deadline.

Covering the city council meetings on Monday night took priority, and many times, they lasted well past nine o'clock, giving me only a few hours on Tuesday morning to finalize the article for our press deadline.

After the babysitter left on Monday night and the kids were fast asleep, I usually sat up till two or three in the morning, scrambling to put a story draft together, giving myself a mental snapshot of how much space I would need for the front page.

Living in Quaker Meadow and working in Apple Butter, I became a member of each chamber of commerce and began expanding my horizons about small-town living. As I got to know the people, my handed-down 'shit-kicker' mentality got replaced with respect for these family-oriented, God-loving citizens.

They were people genuinely concerned about each other and their community. I found a softer, gentler folk than those in New York, and over time I was using the vernacular of "Y'all fixin' to," and my Texas peers were now saying, "Youse guys."

REFLECTING ON THE PAST

Slowly gaining a sense of continuity and stability with a job and a place of my own, I began feeling grateful to God for leading me out of the chaos and suffering I had known in New York. In truth, I didn't go gently. I was more like a willful child, kicking and screaming, "Don't make me go, don't make me go!"

I stayed in New York until the bitter end when the bank foreclosed on our apartment, and I barely had any money left in savings. I waited for an eleventh-hour reprieve from the universe that never came. I didn't want to change. I didn't want to move, but everything around me dictated I must, and I was pissed.

Why is there no punishment for those who deny the truth, not for my now-widowed mother or my ex-husband? Why should I have been the one to move? Why should I have to uproot myself and my children? Why do I have to pay for other people's sins? Why, why, why?

In retrospect, I knew if I groveled for a place back in the family and marriage, I would die a slow soul-sucking death at the hands of my mother and husband, people who, for some reason or another, were incapable of dealing with truth or change.

If I asked to return, pretending none of this ever happened, these same people who once had power and authority over me in their role as parent and husband would treat me as the demon liar they made me out to be.

My husband's cold-bloodedness as to why he lied still shocks me to the core.

So fucking what? What's the big fuckin' deal about what I did? And what are you going to do about it?

If I stayed with him, I would lose something far more valuable than my status in the community and financial security. And so, with less than $2000 in my pocket, two confused little boys, and a sister willing to let us live in her home, I kicked and screamed my way into a new life where change was mandatory and spiritual growth inevitable.

In this new environment, came a new perspective on life. With a growing sense of inner freedom and wellbeing, I began entertaining the idea that moving to Texas was not such a bad idea on God's part. I was embracing thoughts that previously eluded me, allowing me to contemplate life and what it means.

I used to scoff at people who said, 'life is a gift,' a mere platitude because, for most of mine, it didn't feel much like a gift at all. More times than not, it felt painful, threatening, unsafe, and stressful. Worrying was a way of life, and living was something to be endured or avoided with regular escapes into alcohol, food, television, and sleep to keep me going. I lived in the past and future, but rarely in the present. And except for the children, without much joy.

Now in the light of separation, I was gaining some clarity. I began to feel appreciative for getting a spiritual do-over, of becoming more and more aware of my soul. Believing that God knows us even before we're born, and seeing the truth in the psalmist words, "You created every part of me; you put me together in my mother's womb...when I was growing there in secret, you knew that I was there – you saw me before I was born." [1]

I learned the hard way that the moral teaching of my youth concerning the honoring of one's parents and spouses submitting to each other in marriage wasn't mutually shared. Love, or whatever that was, could be withdrawn when the situation suited them. Now I was forced to find another way to live.

My spiritual transformation that day in New Rochelle left no doubt that God is real, and that His Spirit came to me through the wind. I'm still not sure what it meant, or why it happened to me, but I do have a growing sense that God loves me and has welcomed me into His Kingdom as one of His children.

In searching the Bible, I found the Gospel of John. Jesus says plainly, "No one can see the kingdom of God unless they are born again." [2]

He says it twice, but I'm not sure what it means to "see the kingdom" when it's not visible to the human eye?

---

1   Psalm 139
2   John 3:3

My encounter in the parking lot was as accurate as Jesus described to the perplexed high priest, Nicodemus, who couldn't wrap his head around this new life concept either.

"The wind blows wherever it pleases. You hear its sound, but you cannot tell where it comes from or where it is going. So it is with everyone born of the Spirit." [3]

My mind continues to search for answers to why God would give me this new spirit. Was He that voice prompting me to confront my father? If it was, why couldn't He just tell my father to apologize instead of it turning into a nuclear explosion? Maybe I was overthinking the experience. It could be as simple as God coming to my rescue, letting me know he was aware of my situation, arriving just when everything was falling apart. Perhaps, it was a tender reminder that He is my real Father protecting and loving me and that Jesus was the sacrificial gift that paid for this new life of mine. As confused as I was about God's intentions, I found myself amazed at these new insights. Thoughts I could only attribute to the spirit working in my life.

Knowing about and intimately experiencing the Holy Spirit were two very different things. My religion taught that the Holy Spirit was the third person of the Trinity, and there were seven gifts and 12 fruits as a result of the Spirit.

But nowhere in my religious upbringing do I remember hearing that the Holy Spirit could come to me personally. It was a sanctifying means given to the first apostles so they could begin the spread of Christianity after the death and

---

3   John 3:8

resurrection of Christ. If I wanted to share in that sanctification, it would have to come through my connection as a member of the Catholic Church.

No one in my faith claimed to be born again. We were born Catholics and died Catholics with little apostolate fanfare in between.

My numinous encounter left me confused about my identity, leaving me in a spiritual limbo of sorts, dangling between being a life-long Catholic and a budding born-again evangelist. In this puzzling state, I often asked God in the secret of my prayers: *What do you want from me? Give up my children and join a convent? Preach the Good News wearing sandals and a brown robe?*

The experience brought up so many questions. I was still trying to figure out the meaning of salvation and redemption. Does being 'born again' mean being saved and redeemed? I grew up believing I didn't need salvation.

The closest thing to salvation was the weekly confessional box, a kind of gerbil wheel rebirth that allowed a sinner to commit and confess the same sins over and over. And in my mind, redemption was a term reserved for southern tent revivals and traveling evangelists who could save a soul for the price of a ten-dollar admission. The terminology was all very confusing.

In my head, I knew I belonged to God and His Son, but surrendering my will and heart to them both was a bit terrifying. Nobody I knew back home ever expressed a desire to journey with Jesus.

In truth, I was afraid of what God and His Suffering Servant wanted of me. The Jesus who said, "Take up your cross and follow me," was a death magnet and a sure ticket to martyrdom. I wasn't ready to burn at the stake like my namesake. I had suffered enough in New York.

For the time being, I was more comfortable letting Jesus stay on His cross, and I would worship Him from afar rather than entertain any ideas about unconditional surrender and being His disciple.

Except for wrapping fish and moving, newspapers have a short lifespan. But at times, the value of a small-town newspaper can be a keepsake, like when a daughter's full-scholarship to Texas A&M gets published, or a son's athletic prowess lands him a front-page photo as the local sports hero. It's these limelight moments that parents often buy several copies of the paper to send to out-of-town relatives and fill the family scrapbook.

When a beloved store owner gets shot and robbed at gunpoint, readers want the details, not just a blurb that would typically appear in a metropolitan newspaper. And local leaders in small towns realize they have a better platform through a community newspaper because their words and deeds won't get lost or misconstrued by a readership that touts over 100,000, and is not significant enough to warrant a story.

As the sole reporter for the *Weekly Gazette*, I began thinking of myself as adding value and making a difference. I was given entrance into an inner circle of local leadership in both Quaker Meadow and Apple Butter and viewed as a friend and colleague. I got invited to most events around town. And some jokingly referred to me as that 'Yankee, who had her finger on the pulse of both communities.' I looked upon the people's acceptance of me as a gift and was thankful to be part of something larger than myself.

Outside of the local, day-to-day happenings, life at the newspaper came packed with unexpected adventures. It was an exciting world that would have eluded me back in New York. There was the helicopter ride from a local radio station and a hot air balloon ride over Houston from local promoters and free concert tickets that I couldn't afford otherwise.

Having a valid Texas press pass gave me access to most media events in and around the Houston area, including visiting political figures like then U.S. President Bill Clinton, Vice President Al Gore, Republican presidential candidate Bob Dole and then Texas Governor George W. Bush.

My all-time favorite experience was the day retired tennis champion Bjorn Borg came to Quaker Meadow to play a celebrity fundraiser for a young high school student taken ill with leukemia. As an avid tennis fan back in New York, I watched Borg at the US Open with seats so high up, I needed binoculars. Twenty years later, I'm standing in front of him, shaking his hand and taking a front-page photo of him with the young boy he was helping.

This kaleidoscope of events was all part of my small-town living experience in the 90s.

———— ❦ ————

As my outer world expanded with new and exciting adventures, my inner world was under construction, as well.

My old repressed, approval-seeking nature was slowly evaporating under the evolving leadership role the newspaper had given me. And by nurturing my soul through daily prayer, I began growing spiritually, as well, into this new life.

Rising an hour earlier than the boys, I prayed the rosary daily at a small wooden table set up in my bedroom with the same Blessed Mother statue I won in grammar school years ago.

With scented candles, fresh flowers, and a cup of coffee, this regular observance had become my sacred space, giving me time to pray and meditate before embarking on a day filled with long hours and juggling unknowns in the role of a single working mother.

During this morning ritual, I allowed my grief its freedom releasing what would be a steady stream of tears built up from the collective loss that seemed so slow to heal. At times it was difficult to decipher one loss from the other.

Despite all the emotional pain and trauma they caused, I missed having parents. With my father's death and my mother's silence, even after the move, I realized that I was an adult orphan. I laughed bitterly at this self-portrait, realizing its truth and how resentful I still felt over the outcome.

In my mind, the last days of my father's life were supposed to be different. I imagined something reminiscent of a scene from the movie *On Golden Pond*. I was supposed to have closure, one last chance to reconcile with my Henry Fonda father during his final hours here on earth. Without words, all loose ends as his daughter would get tied together in love and forgiveness. A nod of recognition, a look of regret in his eyes, or a gentle squeeze of his hand in mine, some non-verbal disclosure of love before he dies, and then I could enter orphandom with some peace.

Instead, I got silence. And my father's sudden, unrepentant demise felt more like a trap door getting pulled out from under me with his last damning words, "Yeah, but you don't love your mother."

My grief and loss are not without self-blame. I know I pushed the boundary, hoping the seriousness of the accusation would lead to an apology, hoping my father would recognize the wrong he had done. That's all it would have taken for me to heal, but his silence made it worse. Part of me knew my father rarely apologized to anyone, let alone his children. I could forgive his drunkard act, but I had a hard time understanding why, after bringing it to his attention, he couldn't say he was sorry, or have the ability to talk about it.

I blamed my mother for it all, calling me a liar, preventing him from talking to me in the 18 months before his death. But why would she do such a thing? Nothing seemed to make any sense. After his death, there was no time to sort any of this out in my mind. Now through the separation of time, death, and living in another state, the reverence I held for him was losing its luster. I'm beginning to see my father's flaws and weaknesses as they pertain to me; the 'me' whose value for him was lacking because I didn't love my mother.

I'm growing up, maturing, trying to separate myself from the damage that family and marriage caused -- a scary, uncomfortable process that's happening, whether I want it or not.

On one of these prayer mornings, I hear a gentle knock on the bedroom door, a sign that at least one of the boys is awake. They both come in and cuddle next to me on the floor around the prayer table. I get a soft sleepy hug from Brian. Brendan rests his head on my thigh, wrapping his arms around my leg.

The twins are two months shy of their 13th birthday, and over the last year, their harmless roughhousing has become personal, competitive, and at times, downright vicious.

In this quiet early morning hour, the nuzzling begins, predictably leading to a push and ultimately escalating into a full-blown fight. Knowing its sibling rivalry doesn't help. I still find it disturbing, and I'm smack dab in the middle of it. My sister and I were never this vicious with each other.

I've told the children on several occasions, how lucky they are to be twins, to have a brother the same age. And that no matter what happens, they'll always have each other.

Lately, that conversation has fallen on deaf ears. Their sibling rivalry is a daily battle that I'm quickly losing ground on.

Except for once-a-week phone calls, Brian and Brendan have grown up without their father. They have surrogate father figures in their friend's dads who coach football and baseball, and they get invited to plenty of weekend outings.

"But it's not the same as having a real dad," Brendan would say when the subject came up.

Now in the light of my morning reflections and feeling the grief of my father dying so suddenly, I don't want my children to have the same experience and blame me for not knowing their father. It was different four years ago. I was still in a rage over his lies and deceptions. But now I question myself. *Do I have the right to deny them their biological father based on my feelings and failed marriage?*

I silently wrestle with this question. And finally, in the weeks leading up to Brian and Brendan's birthday, I invite the twins' father down to Texas.

THE OLD HERO EMERGES

O ut of the Houston airline terminal comes Bill, looking hot, disheveled, and annoyed. Seeing his wrinkled
beige trousers, scuffed shoes, and hair matted down with
sweat, I'm no longer intimidated by him. Gone is the authoritative swagger that his fake Air Force persona once gave him.

His blonde hair has greyed, and he has grieving lines
around the mouth. The lines say he's aged more than usual
over the last four years. It reminds me of my sister Cathy's
two dogs, Murphy and Tobey, who stayed with each other in
the backyard for over ten years. Last year Murphy died, and
the hair around Toby's mouth grew grey almost overnight.

Suddenly, I feel compassion for Bill, or is it pity? I have a
hard time keeping those two emotions straight. Why should
I feel sorry for him? He signed the divorce papers knowing I
planned to leave New York with the children. He could have
stopped it but didn't. Even now, years later, I feel confused
about him.

He greets us with a pathetic look like he's the victim in
all this, but the boys disarm him with their excitement. He

smiles as they jump into his arms. The three of them are happy to see each other, and that's all that counts right now.

On my part, I feel somewhat in control of my surroundings as I put my best welcome smile on for the man who caused so much devastation. I keep telling myself it's for the boys. They need to be with their father. Maybe his visit will keep them from fighting.

Despite Bill's protests that he isn't drinking, when I give him the ex-wife perfunctory hug, there's a faint whiff of rum coming off him.

Really?

I take a deep breath and walk ahead, praying for the grace to get me through the week. Walking toward the van, Bill sees the "Don't Mess with Texas" sign. And with a sneer of contempt, he flicks his Chesterfield cigarette recklessly toward the dry grassy knoll.

It must be a New York thing.

The smiles on their faces say it was the right decision on my part. I'm happy for Brian and Brendan but less than thrilled with the idea of having their father live at my house for a whole week.

Is this what divorced couples do, have their ex-spouse stay with them while visiting the children they share? Well, maybe if I lived inside the Houston loop, Bill could have stayed at a hotel. But here in sleepy little Quaker Meadow, there are no hotels, and it didn't dawn on him to rent a car.

Money is always an issue between us, and I don't have much sympathy for him. I'm a struggling single-parent who uses food stamps to keep her children fed. I shop at different supermarkets outside of town, so the boys won't be embarrassed if someone from our affluent town sees them when I pull out my food coupons at the checkout. I'm in the era when the stamps have to be torn out at the time of purchase with specific instructions not to fold, spindle, or mutilate, or they won't accept them.

My greatest fear is hearing one of Brian or Brendan's friends say, "Hey, what's your mom got there?" And his cash-paying mother standing behind me tells her kid she'll explain to him later.

My salary at the newspaper covers rent, which is now $600, and the escalating utility bill is almost as high as the rent.

The family minivan breaks down every few months and is regularly in need of an oil change, water hose, or battery. The inner lining on the roof of the van is made of fabric and is always sagging. I've stapled it in place several times to keep it from sticking to the top of my head. The van has no air-conditioning, or if it did, it doesn't work anymore. Barring rain, I keep the windows rolled down. If I drive over 50 mph, the boys and I get a gentle balmy breeze, the kind you get with a hand fan. Stopped at a light or traffic for any length of time, we get drenched by the intense heat and humidity. Despite all the sacrifices, I'm grateful for all I have, including what the boys call our "yabba-dabba doo" car because it gets us to and from school, work, and the different athletic fields.

Having Bill here reminds me of all the financial struggles I've endured for the sake of our children. And it's pissing me off! Rarely does his child support check arrive on time, and many times it bounces, leaving me anxious and fearful of the future.

For his visit, Bill brings cash. I have no frame of reference on how two divorced people are supposed to act for the sake of their children. I've been civil. During the week, I cooked a few meals, and we barbecued a lot. I keep my distance, giving him plenty of time to be with the boys, staying in my room while he shares the bedroom with Brian and Brendan.

One evening I find him sitting outside by himself smoking cigarettes. It's then I see the bottle of rum hiding behind the a/c compressor. In a whispered scream, I confront him so the kids can't hear from their bedroom window above. He says nothing and keeps a tight grip around the bottle, like a dog with a bone, afraid I'll take it away.

The old rage in me rises, and I can't wait for him to leave. Despite my plea of talking to the boys about their fighting, which he says he has done, there's little evidence to suggest any of it.

In my self-contained excitement that he's leaving at the end of the week, I agree to a family trip to Galveston Island for blue crabbing.

Before we leave, Bill wants to stop off at the 7-Eleven so he can buy cigarettes. He can't believe these redneck assholes don't sell Chesterfield non-filters.

I *can't imagine why.*

Oh, and now that I know he's drinking, he shamelessly comes out of the store carrying a six-pack of beer.

Aside from his annoying habit of flicking his cigarette ash out the window, the trip to Galveston starts okay. The boys are happy their father is with them, and I'm thrilled this is the last few days he'll be here. I'm the dutiful ex-wife playing the role of chauffeur.

It feels good to have some control, even if it's only driving this piece-of-crap van. I keep my ambivalence about the vehicle to a minimum fearing it could hear me and break down under the negativity of my thoughts. The van has been good to us, and I don't want to jinx the trip.

In the years here in Texas, I have regular, almost daily growing proof of God's guidance and protection over my life and that of my children. The doors to work, school, even money for the kid's extracurricular activities, doctor's bills, school clothes, and supplies have always opened at the appropriate time with the help of my sister and other sympathetic folks. It isn't the portal of prosperity that I had hoped and secretly prayed for, like winning the lottery, but the doors do open when I need them to.

I'm learning humility, and each instance of need requires a renewed act of faith. In the interim, I spend a lot of time worrying about the future, which, in turn, takes up a lot of my emotional energy. Despite visible signs to the contrary, I'm still not confident in my place with God to think He'll supply all my needs. Admittedly, I'm a slow learner to this new life.

Being around Bill tests my spiritual strength and stamina. In the last year of our marriage with him still struggling to get sober, he suddenly announces he doesn't believe in God or a higher power. In this new epiphany, he also tells me he doesn't want the children raised Catholic or any religion.

"Let them decide for themselves when they grow up," he said, waving his arm in the air.

Shocked by his poor timing since the boys were already going to Sunday school, preparing to make their first Holy Communion, I questioned his motive.

"And this has nothing to do with you not getting sober or finding a higher power?"

"Of course not," he protested.

The boys did make their sacrament that year, but Bill didn't come to the church. Suddenly proclaiming himself an agnostic put another wedge between us. He seemed to get pleasure mocking me, saying what a nice Christian woman I was whenever we got into an argument, and I told him to screw off.

I try to separate the trauma he's inflicted on me as a woman and his wife, and what kind of father he is to Brian and Brendan. It's clear that the boys and Bill love and adore each other, but the jury is still out on what kind of parent he is.

Looking back, his emotional manipulation of me began early and throughout our marriage, and perhaps as far back as DD&B. Did he know back then how insecure I was? In the beginning, he would give me daily compliments, building me up on how beautiful and smart I was, or what a wonderful mother I am. But if he didn't like something I said or did, he would give me the silent treatment, reminding me of my mother.

My Al-Anon friends from New York claim alcoholics are notorious at manipulation and experts at getting what they want. So in light of his new-found agnosticism, I guess he sees no reason to repent for all the wrongs done in our marriage. At times I wonder if he's evil or his booze-soaked brain prevents him from thinking clearly.

I don't like the word, evil. It strikes terror in my heart, and I'm certainly not comfortable putting a label like that onto others. Like goodness, I know it exists, but I can't be sure how it lives in people.

Jesus was comfortable with it. He knew evil's origins and was able to conquer it. He knew its source, and went so far as to proclaim, "No one is good but God alone." He even referred to Peter His disciple as evil, saying, "Get behind me Satan" when Peter tried to talk Him out of going into Jerusalem to meet His death. It seems no one is immune from evil and sin, including parents, "If ye then, being evil, know how to give good gifts unto your children..." [4]

Most of my ideas about the devil come from old movies like *The Exorcist* or *The Omen*. People possessed of actual demons, the bone-chilling scary wet your pants kind, but now I'm thinking evil travels in different ways. It's mysterious, ethereal, and subtle, like someone gently brushing up against you on a crowded street; you never see it coming. It's a living, breathing darkness that exists in all of us.

I prefer to think about the devil on a spectator scale, much like in the movies, because I'm superstitious, believing that the mere thought of the devil will summon him into my life. It's a fear that leads me to ignore it in myself and others, like seeing dog poop on the ground and walking around it. I don't want to step in it.

---

4   Matthew 10:18

My mind returns to the task at hand, loading the Styrofoam cooler filled with sandwiches, juice boxes, soda, chips, and now beer into the van. The blue crab traps made from window screen we bought from the local hardware store bring back memories of my childhood in Edgewater. The boys are eager to test out their new creations. The K-Mart beach chairs are the last things to go in before setting out on this faux family vacation.

It's 10 a.m., and the temperature is already in the low nineties with high humidity. Wiping my brow, I announce that it's 'hotter than blue blazes,' a phrase I picked up from one of my southern neighbors, which results in chuckles from the kids and a quizzical look from Bill.

I'm hoping for light traffic, and once we hit the causeway, the van can sail at 50 miles per hour, and we won't be watching each other sweat through our clothes.

It's only a matter of time before the front axle to the van will break. A warning I received last year from the guy who replaced two of my tires. The axle rubs against the tires, causing the rubber to wear away quickly. A new one costs more than the van is worth, so for now, it's cheaper to replace the tires.

Most of my driving is local, but the clock is ticking on this particular time bomb, and it's a bit of a concern. My anxious mind says going to Galveston is considered a long-distance trip and could be a potential problem, but I throw caution to the wind and put my faith in God.

We are 25 minutes into our destination when I smell something burning. With the windows rolled down, I tell myself the smell is coming from one of the many oil refineries in the area. But the stink of burning rubber follows us, and there's blackish-grey smoke bulging up from the front right side of the van.

Maybe it's one of Bill's Pall Malls caught in a backdraft.

Nope, it's coming from outside. I pull over to the side of the causeway, and we all pile out of the van to watch the flames licking what used to be the front right tire.

Oh, so this is Your plan, God? Being blown up by an exploding gas tank next to my ex-husband -- is this how it all ends?

I pull the boys away from the smoke and watch Bill thrust open the side door to the van, jerking the six-pack of beer out of the cooler. I shoot him a hard look letting him know this is not a "Miller time" moment.

He takes the beer can, shakes it up, and pulls the tab holding it with his two hands like a fire hose. In one giant swoosh, the flames get doused with hops and barley. He does it again with a second can making sure the fire is out. The boys go nuts shouting with glee and pride at their beer-can fireman father.

Shaking my head, I stare at him, then at the melted rubber, and then back again at him.

He looks perplexed. "I'm sorry," he says with all seriousness. "Did you want me to use the juice boxes?"

For a moment, the shadow of the old hero has returned.

A Shift in Perspective

Whether it was the boy's coming of age or weariness on my part trying to keep them from killing each other, Bill's trip that summer was the beginning of a shift in dynamics between the children and me. I never really knew if he tried to instill in them the importance of peace between brothers like he said he would. I only know they fought harder and more frequently after he left.

Until now, I had been avoiding my single-parent status. At times, I felt my singleness in Texas stuck out more than my Bronx accent. Although I had no one in mind, part of me felt uncomfortable opening the door to the possibility of Brian and Brendan having a southern stepfather who might dish out too much discipline or none at all. Or so I told myself.

Truth is after my marriage to Bill, I had no desire to date, but in the aftermath of his visit, maybe having a new man in my life would level the parental playing field and keep the kids from fighting with each other. Perhaps a new guy could make a difference, and the boys would forget all about their father, who left for New York still playing the victim.

I slowly began entertaining the idea that I could have the same happiness I saw in other blended families. The ones I saw watching their kids play sports in the ballfield or enjoying a family meal at the local barbecue place.

At social events, I'm usually third-wheeling with Tracy and Chip, cranking along at the annual chamber and rotary dinners where the crowd, more often than not, is packed with married couples. It's during these times, I feel most alone.

The gender roles in Texas are more defined than in New York. The women I knew back then were very feminine-looking, preferring bright, flowing dresses over slacks. In contrast to yours truly, most of them had long hair, didn't smoke, and rarely used the F-word in public.

In my friendships with them, I learned some valuable lessons on the southern female mystique. These women have big generous emotions on the outside, and rarely get guttural. When gossip about a husband and his infidelity begins circulating, that same woman's ladylike demeanor gets pushed into high gear addressing her curious gossipers with grace and wide-eyed innocence.

"Well, bless his pea-picking heart! He doesn't have enough common sense to stay away from the south end of a northbound skunk!"

A much different approach than I or most of the women up north would have taken.

Maggie was one of those classic southern women. Two years into my tenure, she began selling ad space for the Gazette doing what Tracy did before buying the newspaper.

The paper was growing, and so was the potential for newspaper ads.

Maggie dated and married her high school sweetheart Rory. Her husband not only adored the ground she walked on, but from the look in his eyes, he believed she could walk on water as well. Maggie was a vivacious, confident woman and had a laugh and personality that matched the size of Texas.

After a few weeks at the newspaper, I observed how she could sell underwear to a nudist, especially if that nudist were male. She was a southern yin to my northern yang, and we hit it off almost instantly. So in the presence of two married couples, the pressure was mounting for me to find a date and put an end to what was now fifth wheeling.

There was Jack, who lived in my apartment complex. Jack was a ruggedly handsome man who chewed tobacco and had his own business. He was one of the few single fathers living in the complex, and his son Tyson happened to be friends with my two boys. After football practice, all three pre-teens would go to either apartment to do their homework. In my dating frame of mind, I decided to pick the boys up early one day and get a glimpse of how this southern bachelor lived.

Jack's living room was a hunter's delight. Mounted on the stark white wall was the head of a red stag deer with antlers so massive it took up the entire wall. The taxidermist left enough of the deer's tongue sticking out of its mouth, implying my neighbor might have a strange sense of humor.

On the beige wall-to-wall carpet, lay a bearskin rug with the bear's head and sharp-teeth still intact. The musky scent of animal species was overwhelming.

With this insight into Jack's personality, visions of me in camouflage gear crouched in the woods with a rifle eating beef jerky wasn't my idea of fun. I immediately scratched Jack off my non-existent list of dates.

Tracy and Chip were aware of my dilemma and introduced me to their friend Robb, spelled with two B's as he informed me straight off.

Robb was a transplant from Louisiana whose marriage hadn't survived the move to Houston. When we met, he was a little over a year out of his marriage and had the endearing quality of being unsure of his newly single status. With a full head of dark chestnut hair, a tall, slim build, straight white teeth, and a genuine personality mirroring Gomer Pyle USMC, Robb was easy to look at and like.

My sons instantly hated him. He was the antithesis of their 'real men don't eat quiche' father. Wearing beige khakis, cashmere socks, and black loafers, instead of the usual blue jeans and boots, Robb didn't fit the cowboy stereotype either. I thought I found the perfect blend of north and south.

My need for male companionship is complicated and comes with some ambivalence. I didn't want to go to these socials alone anymore, but quite frankly, the idea of dating again made me want to take a nap. After years of raising the twins and working long hours at the newspaper, I was mentally and physically exhausted. I needed a maid more than a man, but looking at my date-ability meter hedging into midlife 40s, I knew my options were narrowing.

The other side of that coin was wondering if dating was what God wanted. If I belonged to God, could I belong to another human being? Although he wasn't Catholic, Robb spoke positively about his faith and belief in God. The idea of having someone spiritually like-minded in my life gave me hope and the impetus to get my hair done. I decided to test the waters in more ways than one.

***

Wrestling was popular in the 90s, and the boys loved watching it on television. I got free tickets to a live World Wrestling Federation (WWF) match in downtown Houston and invited Robb to come with us, hoping he would escort me to the next rotary dinner with Tracy and Chip, and Maggie and Rory.

The date was a 'love me, love my kids' kind, which in retrospect, I don't recommend, but at the time thought it was a good idea. A public event might be the perfect introduction for Robb to meet the boys.

Personally, I found the sport to be silly -- grown men with ridiculous names slinging their opponents across the ring like rag dolls. But the boys loved it, and anything that kept their hands off each other was a plus. Robb agreed to come as my date, and he would do the driving.

Heading into downtown Houston, the awkwardness of making small talk was made worse by two stony-faced stares coming from the back seat. Brian and Brendan weren't giving him an inch. They listened to every word of our conversation with their steely blue eyes boring holes into the driver's front seat.

As the father of two teenage daughters, Robb was unaccustomed to being around boys and unfamiliar with the sport of wrestling, so he asked them questions hoping to draw them into a conversation. Hearing the excitement in their voices, each trying to outdo the other, showing who knew more than the other by throwing out phrases like *clean finish* and *beat down,* I smiled at this small sign of progress.

Then, the snorts of laughter began.

It took seconds to realize that this pubescent tag team was laughing at Robb's golly and gee-whiz response to their comments. Under their breath, one mimicked him with a fake southern drawl, causing me to cringe with embarrassment. I shot each of them a hard look, hoping that would end their cruel antics. The remainder of the drive into Houston was silent.

Inside the arena, our seating arrangements felt like a wrestling feat of its own getting the boys seated on my right and Robb on my left. If my date knew he was being made fun of, he didn't let on. Nor did he seem bothered by their silence toward him for the rest of the evening.

In a gesture of warmth or nervousness, I couldn't tell which, Robb held my hand throughout the night. During the intermission, we all went to the snack stand, and Robb put his arm around my waist, walking up a set of stairs designed for one person going up and one down. From the look of disgust on their faces, it was clear the boys didn't like my date's public display of affection toward their mother.

So this is what dating someone who eats quiche is like?

Back at the apartment, I sent the boys inside to put on their pajamas while I said goodnight to Robb outside the apartment door. I could hear scuffling and knew one of them was looking through the peephole.

"Oh my God, she's kissing him."

The window to their bedroom on the second-floor slid open, and a water balloon came crashing down on Robb's full head of chestnut brown hair, drowning out any hope of a second date. Robb got a 'beat down,' and I was still fifth wheeling.

Rising Above Our Ditch Paper Status

About a year before I began working at the newspaper, the promise of economic growth had come barreling into Apple Butter. His name was Dwayne Brown, otherwise known as DB, and he was the town's newest city manager.

The city manager form of government dominates the majority of cities and towns in Texas. The role of this appointed official is to run the day-to-day affairs of the administration answering to the elected mayor and city council. But Dwayne Brown's flamboyant managerial style would prove that this small-town visionary, with big ideas, answered to no one.

Dressed in the latest Brooks Brothers suit, Brown's coffee-colored eyes laughed when he spoke, and his quick wit and fast-speech belied his West Texas roots.

Ethnic jokes are unheard of in the south. No one tells Irish or Polish jokes as they do up north. But regional ones are fair game. Quips like: you know you're from Lubbock when you buy a movie rental, ammunition clip, and a bucket of bait all in the same store.

Dwayne Brown was the anomaly of that stereotype, and soon after arriving in Apple Butter, punchlines about his West Texas origins abruptly ended in and around city hall.

With vast tracts of undeveloped land and its proximity to the state highway leading into downtown Houston, Apple Butter was ripe for Dwayne Brown's innovative ambition to transform this rural farming community into a growing metropolis.

His vision for the town was on a grand scale and included the creation of new subdivisions, malls, hospitals, and schools. His infectious enthusiasm toward expansion and growth caught on rather quickly with the residents and local businesses. I was impressed by this man who could talk faster than most New Yorkers and whose southern charm set people spinning on their heels like gleeful children with the prospect of growth and prosperity.

The promise of economic development had an enormous impact on the growth of the newspaper. Each week, I was writing several articles informing the readers of the city's progress toward expansion and the means to make it happen.

City council meetings got lengthier, more involved, and sometimes more heated as those who opposed change voiced their opinions when the city's sweeping fast-track plans got underway. The most highly publicized and hotly debated issue was the proposed bond referendum increasing the local sales tax to pay for all the new roads and infrastructure that would literally pave the way for everything else.

The newly formed City Economic Development Corporation (CEDC) began soliciting businesses in and out of the state, marketing Apple Butter as a smaller Houston with that suburban feel.

To accommodate all the new editorial, advertising, and legal notices coming in, Tracy increased the size of the newspaper from 14 to 18 pages. She also created a new logo for the mast and changed printing press vendors.

Residents who previously had no reason or desire to read the Gazette now had a vested interest and gladly coughed up the 50 cents it cost to buy it.

When publishing the legal notices in both weekly newspapers became too costly, the city put the legal ads out to bid. And in the fall of 1996, Tracy, Chip, and I were summoned to the city manager's office to sign contracts naming the *Weekly Gazette,* as the official newspaper for the City of Apple Butter.

The ever-blistering Texas heat had little impact on our exuberant mood when the three of us pulled into City Hall that day. Walking up the steps toward our destination, I saw our swaggering pride reflected in the glass-mirrored doors leading into the lobby and jokingly referred to us as the 'write stuff.'

Chip's six-foot-tall frame cut a handsome figure with a crisp white shirt, Levi jeans, and calfskin cowboy boots. And the petite Tracy beamed success in her navy blue flared dress with matching red silk scarf. I proudly conveyed a professional image as the new managing editor in a recently bought, just charged, ensemble of black linen slacks with a matching vest and blazer.

The day was the culmination for all our hard work over the last several years, with all three of us personally feeling the infectious excitement of rising above our *ditch paper* status.

Meeting Brown was just a formality. The announcement that the Gazette was the official newspaper for Apple Butter had been made at the last city council meeting. The three of us were there as a formality to sign the contract allowing Tracy and Chip to publish the city's legal notices for a year.

The deal not only symbolized a prestigious step up for the newspaper but had the potential to be a steady stream of lucrative income for the husband and wife team. The Lauder's invitation that I accompany them to the signing was their grateful acknowledgment of my journalistic part in their success.

Dwayne greets us with his usual animated liveliness. His movements and gestures are high energy, suggesting a driven personality, someone who would blend in nicely on the streets of Manhattan.

My eyes scan the room, noticing two freshly-starched white shirts hanging in an open closet, presumably reserved for after-hour meetings and social events. On DB's desk sits a studio-framed headshot of his family, a perfectly coiffed wife, and two equally-coiffed children. I wonder what marriage is like to a guy who moves at the speed of a cross-country train.

Framed in light sandalwood and Feng Shui'd nicely against the dark paneled wall behind his desk, are the city manager's bachelor and graduate degrees, obtained from that place no one is allowed to make fun of anymore.

My thoughts are interrupted when Brown points to the leather couch for us to sit. He offers us a drink from the mini-fridge stocked with a half dozen cans of Dr. Pepper. Knowing it's DB's favorite drink, someone agrees to have one. Maybe it was me, or it could have been Chip, I don't remember. I know all three of us just want to please this new source of income.

As the particulars of the contract move ahead without me, I'm free to scan the room, further sketching out who this powerful man is. I notice he uses his left hand to sign the contract, the same one I use to write.

I ask myself how someone the same age as me gets to be this successful, and almost immediately, I feel a twinge of envy comparing this guy's life to my own.

Why was it so easy for others?

All I wanted was a normal, healthy, married life. But even that simple dream turned into a metaphysical nightmare, making me question everything I previously believed about people and life.

I catch myself falling into the pity bucket and look down at my new clothes and what they symbolize - a promotion to managing editor and a significant pay raise. I have to remind myself how blessed and fortunate I am to be under the grace and guidance of God, who has kept my little family safe. Yes, an unwanted and unexpected journey for sure, but just as the psalmist in the Bible writes, "You know how troubled I am; you have kept a record of my tears... and in the shadow of your wings, I find protection until the raging storms are over."[5]

Despite his southern charm, Dwayne Brown had a ruthless reputation for getting what he wanted. Rumors about him being a loose cannon, of giving pay raises to favored employees without the council's permission and browbeating anyone who opposed him, circulated before I began working at the paper. But by the time I arrived at the newspaper, a new council was in place, and Brown's vendetta against the old one had become yesterday's news.

Knowing his Machiavellian nature, I wonder if the city manager is playing us like pawns on a chessboard.

Does he know? Can he smell our raw, desperate ambition to be a real community newspaper?

Or, is it as simple as him liking us and rewarding us for all the favorable public relations he received and all our hard work in helping the city move forward?

Why did he choose the mom and pop operation over the corporately-owned newspaper? Did it boil down to being the lower bid, or does he have another agenda?

Dwayne looks up from what he's doing. A look in his eye threatens my thoughts, as though he just read them. My

---

5   Psalm 56-57

cheeks flush, a sure indication I've given myself away. The survivor in me quickly rebounds, and I respond with a big bright smile to ease the moment.

I realize Brown is wary of me. I'm confused. It's the same look my history teacher had. In hindsight, the city manager understood the nature of power and control better than anyone of us in that room. As a master strategist, he calculated and weighed the risks before deciding to turn the legal ads over to Chip and Tracy.

Brown knew our livelihood depended on maintaining a favorable relationship with the city and our advertisers. In contrast, our corporately-owned rival, the *Herald-Times,* could go belly up in the area, and would still survive with all the other newspapers they owned throughout Texas. The Gazette didn't have that luxury.

The one variable Brown couldn't foresee in choosing our newspaper was whether or not the power of the pen written by an outsider, a Yankee, was going to work in his favor. Only later would I fully comprehend that wary look on Brown's face.

A Town Touched by Evil

S earching for food to feed her hungry fledglings, the large red-shouldered hawk coils its talons over a scabrous branch. The heavily-wooded area conceals the bird's presence from the unsuspecting frog resting in the marshy soil below.

Preparing to swoop down upon her prey, the hawk casts her proud head back and forth, when a sudden shift in wind threatens her foraged mission. There along the southern corridor of the woods, something far more menacing waits on the dirt road in a dark red pickup.

Following her instincts, the mother hawk circles down and around, hoping her piercing screech, *kee-ahh, kee-ahh,* will frighten the female jogger enough to turn and run in the opposite direction away from the idling truck.

The temperature was a seasonal 62 degrees that spring morning in 1997, weather considered cold by Texas standards, and most of the Quaker Meadow residents would have agreed.

An early riser, 13-year-old Carley Lee Atwater had her day planned. She would run two miles, return home for breakfast, and then break out the books to study. Planning came naturally to the goal-oriented student, who avoided most processed food and practiced yoga as part of her daily discipline.

Her acceptance into the Houston Dance Studio's fall program prompted her recent early morning running routine. Carley planned to spend the rest of the spring and summer building up her leg and calf muscles, giving her the stamina needed for the grueling hours required of a professional dancer. Her new artistic path is why her parents recently agreed to homeschool her, allowing the pre-teen more free time during the day to travel back and forth into Houston.

In 20 days, Carley Atwater would turn 14. In another eight weeks, she would have her braces removed. And in four months, she would be dancing at the academy. But 30 minutes after leaving the house that spring morning, Carley Lee Atwater was gone. She vanished seemingly into thin air, and the gateway to those milestones was gone forever.

Wednesdays begin a new cycle for the newspaper. The Gazette hits the street, and the Lauder's are never in the office that day. Up at the crack of dawn, Tracy's at home rolling newspapers which she stuffs into green plastic polybags that now have the words; the *Weekly Gazette* printed on the outside. She hands the bundles over to Chip, who continues to throw the newspaper to those who live in the most remote parts of town. To my knowledge, no one throws it back at him these days.

As the official newspaper for Apple Butter, and now the City of Quaker Meadow, demand has increased, and so has the circulation. The husband and wife team purchased several vending machines and had them strategically placed near the competition. The Gazette is now at every supermarket and strip mall within the city limits.

With the promise of economic growth, new financial institutions are popping up regularly along the main corridors of both cities, and there is a Gazette vending machine outside every new and established bank, post office, as well as the two city halls.

The vending machines symbolize our rise within the two communities, subtly conveying to our corporately-owned, deep-pocketed rival that our mom-and-pop operation has leveled the competitive playing field in the weekly world of tabloids.

On Wednesday mornings, my brain is on lockdown, and admittedly, I do nothing but show up to the office. With the stress of working all day Monday, followed by the evening city council meeting and then back in the office on Tuesday to put the paper to bed, 'I'm wound up tighter than a two-dollar watch,' as the Texans say.

Sandwiched in between, I have the daunting task of getting two cranky 13-year-olds, dressed, fed, and out the door for what will be their last year of middle school.

As the managing editor for the two newspapers, I'm still writing front-page stories as a reporter, as well as creating headlines, kickers, and cut lines that appear throughout the paper. With the Gazette growing, Tracy has hired a couple of part-time stringers who pick up the slack and go to the police departments to create *Police Beat*, a weekly column that gives a rundown of all the petty crime that occurred in the area for the week. What isn't petty gets fleshed out and written as a news article. It's my job to edit all copy that comes in. In my new position, I get to expand my journalistic horizons to include editorials, book reviews, human interest, and special-feature writing when space allows.

On Wednesdays, my head is a liquid pile of nothing. I confine myself to simple tasks that don't require much effort. Answering the telephone and splurging on a big lunch with the rest of the staff falls into that category.

The rest of the full-time team consists of Maggie and Taylor. Maggie's southern charm continues to sell ad space to a new wave of steady advertisers who've jumped on the economic-growth bandwagon. With Adobe Photoshop, Taylor creates the ads, mostly from scratch, and is responsible for laying out the newspaper on Tuesday with Tracy.

With only half the staff, we speak with pride at publishing a weekly product equivalent to our rival. Tracy and Chip's flexibility as owners sits favorably with our readership. No one gets turned away with a last-minute request for an ad or a letter to the editor.

On one particular Wednesday, Tracy receives a phone call at home from Bonnie, who works at the chamber of commerce. Bonnie tells her that 13-year-old Carley Lee Atwater has gone missing for almost four hours, and the family is frantic. *Missing* is code for runaway, kidnapped, or worse. Bonnie asks Tracy if I can go and meet with the family and write a story to get the word out.

There's no right or wrong way to react to the news that a child is missing. Everyone's reaction is different. Initially, I wasn't shocked. I was leaning more toward dispassion, an emotion I picked up that first month after those two little girls got murdered by their father. It took months to get past their screaming voices heard on that 9-1-1 tape and me sleeping on the floor of my children's room at night, believing I was keeping them safe.

Despite being the same age as Brian and Brendan, I didn't know Carley Atwater or her family. Homeschooling precluded any opportunity to meet the young girl's parents, even if it was to exchange a smile in the hallway at a school open house.

Though my cub status is behind me, I still walk a fine line between putting my personal feelings and opinions into a story and keeping it professional and detached. So now, my current mantra is, "Just the facts, ma'am."

But as the events of the day unfold, it's clear the situation is not some pre-teen running away from home or disobeying her parents by skipping school to be with a wayward boyfriend. Something happened out of the ordinary, outside the natural flow of life that spring morning in 1997.

Once again, an outsider would brazenly challenge the safety of our Norman Rockwell environment, slashing its picture-perfect portrait into contemptible shreds testing our notions that nothing like this ever happens in our town. But this time it did and to one of our own.

"You expect this kind of thing to happen in big cities like Houston," I would hear. "Even Apple Butter," someone said sardonically, "but not Quaker Meadow."

My thoughts leave me feeling vulnerable. If this could happen to a child with two parents at home, then it could feasibly happen to two little boys with one parent living in an apartment complex. After years of living in the community, my cautious New York nature would never allow me to keep the apartment door unlocked, though it's common here in Quaker Meadow.

But what happened to Carley wasn't about locked doors, or having two parents. Those were rational explanations trying to make sense out of something insensible. What happened to Carley Lee Atwater was a deliberate act of evil, from being in the wrong place at the wrong time, created by seemingly random events that came together, culminating in tragedy.

By the time I sat down with Carley's parents that afternoon, the community had begun rallying around the family. In a little over 24 hours, the Quaker Meadow police and fire department, and hundreds of volunteers came forward to help in search of the missing girl.

My job that day was to give two frantic parents an outlet and tell me who Carley was. We sat on the front porch of their home that spring afternoon, and it was here I learned of their daughter's plans to become a professional dancer, her love for family, and her determination to reach her goals.

The Gazette headline would read, "Carley Lee Atwater, the Community's Child."

A week passed with no word. The number of volunteers from Quaker Meadow and the surrounding areas grew even more. Fort Hood reservists scheduled for field exercises that week came to Quaker Meadow instead, to search the surrounding wooded areas.

The case received city, state, and national attention, culminating 17 days later when they found Carley's naked sexually assaulted body in a drainage ditch, less than 15 miles from her home. Her tragic death would change the emotional landscape of a city whose spiritual mettle had never been tested with evil like this before.

My final headline the week of Carley's funeral would read, "A Community Mourns Their Child."

In the weeks following the Atwater murder, my mind once again dwells on the nature of evil and darkness. In the aftermath of writing about two gruesome crimes involving the slaughter of children, here in Texas, I've become acutely aware that wickedness is part of our human existence, even in the safest of places.

My experience teaches me that evil does exist, and it shouldn't be looked upon lightly or ignored like that poop on the sidewalk. It's personal and surrounds everything we do, every decision we make. It comes at us through the actions of other human beings, striking at any time, waiting to destroy, maim, or in the very least, doubt the goodness of God.

The fact that God allows Satan to roam free is well documented. The Devil is part of God's free will package we inherit at birth. To be given a choice between right and wrong, good and evil, all sounds simple enough. But, I'm beginning to think that God gives His creatures too much credit for doing the right thing and perhaps, way too much freedom. Some of His 'children' shouldn't have free will at all, but who am I to dispute the hidden wisdom of God.

Yet, God knew what these murderous men were going to do. He should have stopped it from happening. Why didn't He? Why did God allow those innocent children to die?

It's easy to rail against the goodness of God. Our lives are continuously asking similar questions about events in our own experience, like how God can allow a mother to casually damn her daughters for being liars because she refuses to hear the truth. Or in a former spouses' *what's a few drinks* expression when he came to visit, pretending his drinking had nothing to do with the divorce. Our lives continuously challenge God's goodness, weighing it against the inevitable tides of death and loss that ebb and flow in our daily living.

A husband enraged by his wife leaving him, murders his children in revenge, shattering the world they created. A stranger sees a young girl and, for reasons only he knows, annihilates her. The cycle of darkness begins: faith is lost, survivors are born, life becomes harder, evil laughs, and goodness weeps. How do we guard against such evil?

To fight the good fight as my Christian roots teach, I must understand who and what I'm struggling against. To be that *Soldier of Christ*, a phrase that now comes to mind from my fifth-grade rite of confirmation, I have to understand spiritual warfare, and that requires much more than a bishop's slap on the cheek.

Jesus tells us that it's in the heart where all darkness takes place, where the seed of all sin gets planted.

"For out of the heart come evil ideas, murder, adultery, sexual immorality, theft, false testimony, slander." [6]

It seems a heart without love cannot withstand the onslaughts from the devil, and as humans, we can easily be swayed by all the negativity in the world, preventing us from living fully in God's love. Acknowledging this spiritual truth is part of my growth and maturity brought home by the death of Carley Lee Atwater.

I'm still not sure how to approach this new life. What do I do with this new perspective? I can't pretend that this spiritual birth never happened. As I've grown to understand it, I'm a seven-year-old child confined in a 42-year-old adult body learning how to navigate this new inner world. It's a journey that comes with a variety of wonder, joy, grace, ambivalence, pain, struggle, and loneliness. And in this growth process, God readily challenges me on any predictable premise I think I have about Him or my life.

---

6   Matthew 15:19

It's frustrating to be indebted to God for my very survival because reliance on anyone doesn't come naturally for me. My will is always trying to exert itself, and I struggle against the total dependence I believe He wants me to have on Him.

Things Fall Apart

B rendan looks up at me and says, "I want to live with Dad. He needs me."

The words from his mouth are clear and precise. There's no hesitation in his young, adolescent voice when he repeats the same two sentences as though I didn't hear them the first time.

I look down at my soon-to-be 14-year-old son in silent shock and witness the pain in his eyes when he speaks about his father living all by himself in New York.

Oh yeah, your poor remorseless father, who knows how to manipulate any situation to his advantage.

The fear of losing either of my sons through death and murder, like Carley Lee Atwater, barely had time to scab when Brendan announced he wanted to move back to New York to be with his father.

I don't know what shocked me more, the unwavering surety in his tone, or the fact that he could up and leave Brian and me without so much as a blink.

Brendan would be 14 in another ten days, and I found it oddly disturbing that someone so young could make that kind of cognitive decision on his own. I was sure all those late-night phone conversations he had with his father over the summer had something to do with it.

I can almost hear Bill promising Brendan how great it would be, just the two of them, father and son, mutually bonding over the masculine things that real men do. No quiche-eaters please -- only swashbucklers need to apply.

As his mother, it was gut-wrenching news, and the painful reality of his rejection was only beginning to set in. The sacred bond of maternal love that brought Brendan into the world, promising to nurture him through infancy, walking with him through every step, clapping, laughing, and crying at all his incredible feats of accomplishment seemed to snap like a dried twig under the light of this rejection.

Perhaps his decision is the result of a broken home where kids tend to grow up faster, a plausible thought of mine that hadn't made it to my heart yet.

The boys were two weeks into their freshman year of high school. I wanted to believe that their intense fighting was just a passing phase of adolescence, and entering high school would change all that. Finding out from the guidance counselor that Brendan was crying in her office those first two weeks only added to the shock of the situation. I had no idea how unhappy he was, and losing him to his father was equally heartbreaking and confusing.

What did I do wrong?

Brendan didn't adjust as well as Brian to southern living. Of the two, I expected Brian to be the one moving back to New York. Brian was a free-spirit and made friends easier than Brendan. Brian was outgoing, adaptable, and comfortable in almost any social environment. Brendan was a fearful child, full of anxiety, and worried over the smallest of changes.

On shopping trips to the local Wal-Mart, Brian went off to the electronics department playing the latest video games until I had to drag him away when it was time to go. Brendan was the opposite. He never let me out of his sight and followed me through the aisles, acting as though I might abandon him.

As a baby, Brendan was the one who required the most attention. He was bright, curious, and spoke intelligently beyond his years, and was emotionally demanding of my time. Brendan vied for my attention like it was a competitive event against his brother. Brian, on the other hand, was laid-back, kind, and considerate who most times waited patiently for whatever time he and I could share.

I loved both Brendan's need for me and Brian's independent spirit. Raising the boys alone was always a challenge, but I believed that the long-term rewards would outweigh the struggle. I thought if I promoted peace and brotherly love between them, they would eventually appreciate the gift of being twins.

It would just take time and maturity to understand how fortunate they were to have each other - another family paradigm of mine that crumbled under the weight of being tested.

I have sole custody of the twins and am not legally obligated to let Brendan go. I never asked Bill why he didn't protest my leaving New York and just assumed he thought I was bluffing. His child support payments aren't as vital as they once were since my promotion and a higher salary. If I fought Brendan on this, he would resent me for not allowing him the opportunity to know his father, and the fighting between brothers would most likely escalate.

Brian seemed okay, maybe even slightly relieved, with the idea of his brother going to New York. Perhaps, it was the best thing all around, for the time being.

Knowing his fears, I try to imagine Brendan attending one of the local public high schools in New York, where metal detectors were now the new norm. My heart pounds at the thought, and I further weigh the consequences of my son's demand. After discussing my concerns with Bill, he promises to put Brendan into private school and ease up on the drinking.

Maybe having Brendan in his life will motivate Bill to go back to AA. Perhaps this move isn't such a bad idea, after all. School up north would be starting in September, and with his adamant refusal to listen to my pleas, I felt there was little to do but prepare Brendan for his new journey.

I felt shattered by this impending loss, at the thought of another change to my already disintegrating family life. The twins were my motivating force, the reason for living, and the source of all my love. Our move to Texas was supposed to be a fresh start for all of us, giving the children a healthy environment filled with solid community values and activities they could imitate and incorporate into their adult lives. This latest development wasn't how life was supposed to turn out.

The memory of driving Brendan to the airport still remains a blur. I don't remember much, only telling him how much I loved him and that he could always come back home if things didn't work out. I wanted him to be happy, but almost immediately after he boarded, a familiar sense of loss and depression took hold. I was starting to feel the tragedy of life come upon me once again.

Not long after Brendan left for New York, I started drinking alone. It wasn't something conscious on my part; it just began. Brian would be off with his friends, and I'd be home alone watching television, or talking in chat rooms on the computer, drinking a glass of wine or two to dull the pain of losing my son.

I drank to drown out the uncomfortable questions that began circulating in my head about God and His goodness. The loss of Brendan to his father was the beginning of my doubt that God was looking out for my best interests. Why, after all these life-altering changes in marital and economic status, why would this be the outcome? I soon regretted letting Brendan go, and as the doubts in my head grew louder, my drinking steadily increased.

The inner turmoil was growing darker, more harmful, overshadowing the positive light I had known up until then. I slowly drifted away from my daily prayer life, finding excuses not to pray. Passively angry at God, I convinced myself He was punishing me through my son for not committing entirely to His will. I felt let down by the very spirit I was obediently trying to follow. And eventually, the idea of handing my will over to God, letting Him be in the driver's seat, became too much work. In the daily grieving for the loss of my son, I felt prayer wasn't worth the effort.

Rumors had been swirling for months that City Manager Dwayne Brown was up to his old tricks at Apple Butter City Hall. Proof surfaced that Tuesday morning when a disgruntled councilman called the Gazette to leak some startling news: in a closed-door session, the City Council voted 3-2 to delay DB's annual pay increase over concerns about his job performance.

Not long after that phone call, a copy of Brown's confidential performance review mysteriously appeared over the newspaper's fax machine.

The jaw-dropping performance review accused DB of overstepping his authority and verbally abusing staff members, going as far as threatening to fire uncooperative employees – including the city attorney who questioned the legality of some of Brown's past and present land deals.

Here was the real story. It was no secret that Dwayne Brown belonged to the local Pentecostal church and had several of its church members sitting on the newly-formed planning and zoning board, helping to pass the city manager's progressive agenda.

One such deal was the purchase of several hundred acres of farmland earmarked as a future major highway in and out of Apple Butter. The Pentecostal church purchased the land ahead of time, presumably knowing the city's eventual plans to build a road and then resold the farmland back to Apple Butter for an immense profit, leaving a conflict of interest stain on Brown's reputation.

Without solid proof that the city manager was involved, but speculation growing from his hostile behavior toward city employees questioning his methods, the internal campaign to get rid of Dwayne Brown began.

Despite the accusations against him, Brown had become the city's economic savior. Over the last several years, he gave Apple Butter a new face and identity as a modern, growing metropolis where aging yuppies working in downtown Houston would want to move and start a family. Where large out-of-town businesses being eeked out by high rents and property taxes would get a better tax deal if they moved to Apple Butter. And with the building of new schools and hospitals, the creation of hundreds of jobs made people rethink this once undeveloped farming community. Through his leadership, DB turned a country bumpkin town into a prosperous reality.

When word got out that Brown's reputation was once again in question, this time of him violating a deeply held conviction in the separation of church and state, the floodgates of public opinion reopened, forcing residents to decide which side of the political fence they wanted to be on.

Knowing this kind of story could put the newspaper in jeopardy when the legals contract came up for renewal, I immediately brought the information to Tracy and Chip. They would have to decide whether or not to run the story. Although never discussed, we all knew that Brown could be vindictive and would have no problem refusing to renew the newspaper's contract when the time came.

Adding to our dilemma was the acknowledgment that the same information was getting faxed over to our competitor, who had nothing to lose financially. The situation would push the Gazette between an ethical rock and a hard place for the first time since its existence. With the paper going to press that afternoon, a decision had to be made and made quickly.

Until now, the Gazette and the city were as compatible as a plate of chicken-fried steak covered in gravy. Over the last few years, there was nothing close to controversial in my weekly reporting on the city's progress of attracting new industries, big and small, into Apple Butter, calling it their home. It was all 'feel good' news. Admittedly, my writing was taking on more of a business style than a journalistic one, but with the readers focused on the Atwater murder in Quaker Meadow, no one complained or seemed to notice.

Not wanting to be accused of partisanship, the Lauders' decided to run the story, telling me to keep the writing neutral and place it under the fold for less exposure. In the newspaper world, the placement of a front-page story above the fold indicates it's the lead story, anything below the fold is considered secondary.

Despite its placement, the no pay-raise story got noticed, opening up a floodgate of trouble for Brown, who seemed to be a lightning rod for this kind of controversy. As more and more information about him and his ties to the Pentecostal church emerged, people who didn't believe mixing religion with politics came forward voicing their concern, especially those who weren't part of that Pentecostal denomination.

DB's last-ditch effort to shut down the rumor mill came when he walked into the office and threatened to pull all the city's advertisers, including the legal ads, and give it to the Herald.

Standing near my desk, the emotionally charged city manager glared over at me, making it clear to Tracy and Chip he wanted a retraction or me gone from the newspaper. Knowing we could never print a disclaimer for what was now the truth, it was clear DB wanted a scapegoat for his problems and who better than someone expendable, someone not born and bred in the great state of Texas?

Over the next several months, Brown used his political influence to get some of his cronies to pull their advertising from our newspaper. He continued his threats to cancel the city's legal contract as a pressure tactic for Tracy and Chip to fire me. In the face of such pressure, the Lauders were gracious and unyielding.

Eventually, I handed in my resignation, telling Tracy and Chip I was moving back to New York, a gesture that the relieved couple gladly accepted. Over the years, the Lauders and I became good friends as well as colleagues. I was grateful for their loyalty and friendship, especially in the last months of my tenure as managing editor.

After I left Texas, Chip sent me copies of the newspaper every week to keep me in the loop. Three months after returning to New York, I read that Apple Butter finally terminated Dwayne Brown as its city manager, but not without giving him a lucrative payout. Although not disclosed, the amount must have been considerable for him to remain in Apple Butter and stay living in his five-bedroom house.

In another issue a few weeks later, a photo op of Brown with members of the Apple Butter Chamber of Commerce appeared announcing the opening of DB's new real estate firm on the outskirts of town. I just laughed at the irony of it all.

"And you shall know the truth, and the truth will set you free."

JOHN 8:32

THE RETURN HOME

I missed Brendan terribly and believed he would eventually get tired of living with his father and would want to move back home. That didn't happen.

The fear of losing him forever if I stayed in Texas, working at another job, was the motivating factor to return to New York. I wanted my little family of three back and reasoned if the three of us couldn't be in the same house, I would settle for being in the same state.

Brian and I landed at LaGuardia Airport that Christmas morning in 1999. The flight attendant announced the temperature as a frigid 19 degrees. Neither mother nor son felt prepared for the drastic change in temperature or environment.

During the flight, I tried to quell Brian's fears about this significant change in lifestyle, telling him that living with his father for the first time and reuniting with his brother would be a good thing.

"You'll get to know your dad, just like Brendan is doing now," I said, stroking his thick blonde hair and trying to sound confident.

The decision to move back to New York weighed heavily on my mind and came with a lot of doubt and uncertainty. I never prayed over it, asking God if this was the right thing to do. I just packed everything up and stayed the course.

Well, at least this time, it's my choice.

I was still a bit confused about Bill and his attitude toward parenting. Before the divorce, he rarely spent quality time with the boys saying once they were out of diapers, he would get involved, and then it was once they got into grade school. He always had an excuse, and then, the marriage was over. Despite my concerns, I want to be fair and impartial.

Did I have the right to deny Brian the other half of his biological makeup because of my bias toward him? Didn't Brendan move to New York because he needed a father? From my conversations with him, Brendan seems to be doing quite well, adjusting to his new surroundings and in a new school. Maybe, I was too harsh on my ex-husband.

The conversation about alcoholism came up early for the boys. In Texas, as they got older, I spoke to them at length about how alcohol addiction is a family disease and that there's alcoholism on both sides of the family. I cautioned them about drinking when they got older because children of alcoholics are more than likely to become alcoholics themselves.

Despite what I believe about his drinking problem, Bill is by all appearances doing well financially, living in a $2500 a month three-bedroom home in Westchester with an excellent school system. Brendan is in his second year of a private school where the tuition is five digits. His drinking doesn't seem to interfere with his ability to provide a home and education for his son. Maybe he did stop or cut down on his drinking.

Living with his father and brother, Brian will be able to finish out his last two years of high school in an upscale school system similar to the one he had in Texas, or he can go to private school. I tell Brian that everything will work out, but I'm not sure of either of our fates.

I'm going to live with my mother. Admittedly, yes, it's a half-assed plan with many unknowns, but I tell myself it's only temporary until I can find a job and make enough money to get a place of my own. That's the unknown part. Rents are much higher, and the $500 I got for a two-bedroom in Texas isn't enough to rent a room here in New York. But I keep telling myself, at least the children and I will be in the same state.

Despite my worries about the move, I'm overwhelmed with hopeful expectations looking down at the bright lights surrounding the airport runway and around the bay as we get ready to land. I realize there's comfort in the familiar, no matter what that familiar is.

As Brian and I head toward the baggage area, I hear the distant sound of *Oh Holy Night* reminding me it's Christmas Day. Nostalgic memories of better days well up in me, feel-good memories knowing that no matter what the budget was that year, we managed to have a real Christmas tree full of knotty pine smells adorned with strings of bright lights. Food and baked goods were always in abundance, and no one was disappointed in what Santa left under the tree. I hope this year's Christmas and the new year will be every bit as memorable.

Watching the crowds of families, young and old, pass by in a cinematic blur, I'm amazed at the number of people who travel on this day. They all look excited to get to their destination. I wish that were my feeling.

I drag the luggage closer toward the exit, so it will be easier for Bill to find us when he comes. He'll drop me off at City Island before taking Brian to his new home. The plan is to celebrate Christmas with the boys the next day, giving everyone a chance to settle in.

Waiting for our ride, Brian and I get an unexpected jolt from some asshole who kicks our luggage out of his way so he can get to a waiting limo.

"Merry Christmas!" I shout.

He acknowledges my yuletide gesture with one of his own. Mother and son enjoy the last laugh they will have for a while.

In contrast to the other brightly lit homes on the block, my parents' house on City Island is in darkness. It looks gloomy and worn. There are no festive holiday lights, Frosty the snowman, or Rudolph and his reindeers, welcoming me or any of the drive-by families who make it a yearly tradition to check out the decorated homes on the island. There's no evidence to suggest who we are on this holiday season. And if I didn't know better, I'd think the house was vacant.

The wood trim above the garage is rotting with age. The cement sidewalk has several deep cracks leading down into the driveway giving further proof of the home's exterior decline. With a depressed sigh, I notice the same green plastic wreath with its missing holly berries over the door, a remnant from Christmases past. The lion's head door knocker remains proudly in its place, and I use it to let my mother know I have arrived.

Stepping inside feels like a time warp. The white walls with gold stencil now have a yellow tinge overlay from age and nicotine, a visible reminder that the house needs painting. The gray fiber-mesh couch and love seat smothered in plastic, sit in the same spot in the living room as they did in the 70s. And the russet-colored rug, with its long lost shag, holds the same rank smell of cigarette smoke as the rest of the house.

The only light on in the house is a dim bulb over the kitchen sink. Walking toward the kitchen, I notice the same comforting nativity scene sitting on the credenza from years ago. Next to it, a small white ceramic tree with little blue lights sticking out of the holes has replaced the balsam fir Daddy used to put up and decorate every Christmas.

The red and green eyelet curtains on the kitchen window look new, tangible evidence of change, but even they strain against this melancholic atmosphere. A dry, sagging poinsettia sits hopelessly neglected in the kitchen corner, and a wrinkly vinyl tablecloth with a plastic pine-cone centerpiece from ten years ago completes this Yuletide snapshot.

With a deep sigh, I welcome myself home.

Phone negotiations between my mother and I began three months before my return to New York. The nature of these conversations took on a tense political tone between two opposing forces rather than a daughter's simple request to return home until she got back on her feet.

Knowing I need a good reason, I touch on Ma's fear of being alone, promoting my value to her now that Albert is in the hospital dying of leukemia. Albert is Ma's 'boyfriend,' a word I find as distasteful as soap in my mouth.

Over the years, my mother's nervous condition kept her from driving. It was a pre-existing condition dating back to our Edgewater days and got further inflamed by my father's lack of patience when he tried to teach her to parallel park. Traumatized, she ran back in the house in tears, vowing never to get behind the wheel again. Not getting her driver's license was one of those missed milestones that created another layer of marital co-dependency between her and my father, who drove her everywhere.

As I saw it, Mother's peccadillo worked in my favor. If I had any hope of returning to New York, getting on my feet, and having my little family back, I had to promise I would take care of her. And that meant driving her to the hospital to see Albert, take her shopping, to the doctors, and of course, helping out with the bills once I got a job.

I have no problem taking care of my aging mother. I do have an issue in the continuous way she treats me. But because I need her, I convince myself I can overlook our past. I tell myself I've matured and grown tremendously over the last several years. I'm stronger from my wilderness experience and feel empowered by overcoming the strains of a broken marriage, being homeless, and finding a new home and career in a community that was good to me. I tell myself, for the love of my children, I can climb that mountain again.

The second phone call I made before leaving Texas was to my ex-husband. Since Bill had plenty of room in his rental house and lived in a community with an excellent school system, I reasoned Brian could live with him while things got sorted out. I gave him the deliberate impression that I was rethinking our relationship using phrases like 'doing what's best for the boys' and 'maybe we just needed some time apart.' I even convinced myself that it could be true.

Wanting to resume the memories with my little family of three so bad, I surprised myself at how easy it was to slip into a deceptive mode. I was vaguely aware of doing the same thing Bill tried to do with me before I left New York, pretend that nothing had changed.

My relationship with God has taken a hit. I don't ask Him what He wants of me anymore, nor do I pray every day the way I did in Texas. That stopped about a year ago. The joy from that luminous moment in the parking lot has faded bitterly under the glaring reality of life and its disappointments. I'm alone with a plan of my own; however, muddled that idea seems to be. The seed of my new life has dried up, and its thorns have me in a chokehold. Renegotiating my truth for a place to sleep doesn't make me feel very spiritual anyway. I tell God, *c'est la vie*, hoping He understands my decision. His way just wasn't working, and for the time being, we're going to try mine. For now, the wine is working. And that's good enough for me.

Drinking prevents me from addressing the inner wall of agony, pain, and bitterness that keeps building up over my emotionally ruptured world. Like bathwater that can be warm, sometimes scalding, the liquor soothes and deadens the raw homicidal emotions festering inside me, maniacal thoughts, that if acted upon, would put me in a prison cell or a straitjacket. The alcohol keeps these dark emotions at bay so I can focus on going to work and pretend everything's normal.

An Abyss of
Dysfunction

Two years have come and gone, and I'm still living with my mother on City Island. The boys graduate high school in a few weeks.

I've set up a mini-office with a phone and computer in the basement so I can work on my real estate activities. I laugh at the irony. The basement is the same place where my father used to drink his beer and listen to music. Now, I'm doing the same thing.

The turntable/8-track player is still here, along with my father's old record collection. I've added a television, a small couch, and some new curtains to the downstairs. I drink wine at night in front of the computer and talk in chat rooms until I pass out in the swivel chair.

I work for a commercial developer and have a license to sell real estate. Any romanticized vision I had of myself fighting the evil forces through the power of the pen is no longer on my list of things to do. Money is my motivational god.

The paycheck I now take home would allow me to live quite nicely in Texas, but $40k here in New York barely covers rent for a studio. I've morphed into a realist putting the children on my medical and dental insurance, providing the braces and eyeglasses they need. I give rent money to my mother and pay my ex-husband for added expenses. With Brian and Brendan both graduating high school, this last year has been costly. Two of everything is needed: class photos, yearbooks, senior rings, and prom expenses.

During this same period, it's clear I'm no longer the dominant parent, the hands-on mother enjoying the presence of her children, helping with homework, and watching them play sports on weekends. My parental influence and authority have been overshadowed, at times obliterated, by my lack of presence in their daily lives. I drive up on weekends, take them to doctor's appointments, teach them to drive, and go to parent-teacher conferences. But whatever parental authority I had, has waned in the presence of their father's parenting skills, which resembles a free-for-all, a live and let live kind of lifestyle. Bill wants to be their friend and not their father, a preferred parenting method the boys seem to enjoy.

Their household has gone into a chaotic disintegration worthy of any Jerry Springer show with all the pizza boxes and empty soda bottles piled up, dirty clothes in every room, a broken toilet, and dishes piled in the sink. Two jousting swords lie on the floor, evidence of their playful banter from the night before.

A rock glass with rum and a splash from the previous night sits in a watery pool on the living room coffee table. More alarming are the empty liquor bottles that don't get hidden anymore when I come up. Bill's drinking has become carelessly defiant, evolving into a morning routine. He seems to blame me since I rebuffed all attempts to reconcile.

In the beginning, I tried not to let the past interfere with the present. But I soon realized that much of Bill's attraction for me was that he claimed to be a man of substance and character, a man who lived with courage, honor, and integrity. As long as he was that Air Force paratrooper jumping out of airplanes in his head, or could hold onto the illusion of being that golden knight, he could transform himself into that courageous man of substance he so wanted to be, to himself and others. But without the lie, he had no identity. He was this lost soul without a core, and that scared me the most.

Our inability to reconcile ended any friendly talk that went on between us. Bill denies making derogatory comments to the boys about me, but our lack of marital reconciliation coincides with the children's growing detachment. Once again, I've become an outsider, but this time in my own family.

His insistence that everything is okay increases the insanity of his drinking. He claims he's working, but making phone calls from the house and not going into the office isn't working. His body seems to have shrunk from weight loss and poor nutrition, and what used to be a robust set of muscle mass on his upper arms has now turned into atrophied skin. The slogan I heard in Al-Anon, "the denial is worse than the disease," is certainly true in this case.

I'm aware of my own growing dependence on alcohol compelling me to buy a bottle of wine or two, even when I consciously don't want to. It's the same force that has taken complete control over my ex-husband, and I shudder at this mental snapshot of what could lie ahead for me if I continue to drink.

I quickly dismiss this thought in light of Brian and Brendan's plight of watching their father's slow descent into his disease and the anxiety of not knowing what will happen from one day to the next. It's heartbreaking for me to think about how the boys have now become their father's caretaker, and the guilt I feel for putting them in this toxic environment.

Life with my mother has evolved into an uncomfortable comfortableness with long stretches of silence between us. After working all day in Connecticut, I drive to Westchester for my second evening job, renting apartments in and around White Plains.

This second job, at times, can be lucrative. Rents have risen dramatically over the last few years, and a one-bedroom apartment can lease for as high as $2,000. Commission for a rental is good, usually 40 percent of the first month's rent. But competition for listings is fierce and can be cutthroat at times, making commission payments unpredictable. I have access to the realtor's multiple listing service, letting me know what new listings have come on the market.

After working long hours, I sometimes go out with the other realtors for a few drinks. If not, I stop off at the liquor store to buy a bottle or two of wine before heading home. I avoid going to the same liquor store every night, so the cashier doesn't suspect I have a problem.

Sometimes I buy my alcohol in Connecticut, conveniently located next to a supermarket where I can pick up a few groceries and then head into the liquor store and act like someone searching for the perfect cabernet to have with dinner. The problem with that storyline is most times, I don't eat dinner and have more than a glass or two of cabernet.

For the last few years, I've kept my promise being Ma's caretaker, driving her to and from the hospital waiting for her beloved Albert to pass away from leukemia. At Albert's funeral, I get to meet his family and, most notably, a bubbly married niece named Kyra that Mother fawns over with uncharacteristic kindness and affection. I'm amazed at this side of my mother because I've never experienced being fawned over by her.

Growing up, she always found something to praise in my girlfriends, how nice, intelligent, funny, pretty, or kind they were, leaving me wanting for a compliment of my own, but it never materialized. Back then, children didn't receive praise from their parents because of the belief it would make their head swell with pride, or so I was told. But now, I'm seeing Mother's behavior in a whole different light. I realize her actions are calculated and deliberate.

It's just one of the many things I find disturbing about her living in the same house. My relatively easy-going nature has a hard time connecting with her hard-core temperament. I see things in her personality and character that eluded, confused, and hurt me when I was younger, situations I didn't have words to describe.

But now at 49, I realize something's mentally wrong with her. She lies about almost everything, either by omission or most times, for no reason at all. It's incredibly distressing that my septuagenarian parent hasn't outgrown her insensitive, self-centered ways.

After enduring a harrowing divorce that left me homeless, it's soul-crushing to live under the same roof with someone who offers no emotional support, sympathy, or downright concern for all I've gone through. Instead of being outrageously indignant, even somewhat appalled by what my ex-husband did to me and support me in my decision to divorce him, I get, "What's a few lies?"

Even more infuriating, she continues to send him cards for his birthday and on Father's Day, as she did when we were married. It's her philosophy that no matter what she says to offend, a card from her always ends with "All my love, mom."

Buying her a card is an obligatory madness. I'd rather punch myself in the face than go to the store to choose from the mawkish selection of Mother's Day cards that dictate how I'm supposed to feel as opposed to my real feelings.

The turning point in my patience comes when her caustic comments focus on Brian and Brendan: what they should wear and how they should act or behave. Her growing criticism of them is the last straw, and I resolve to move out after they graduate high school.

Until then, the thing that keeps me sane is drinking. I find that a nice bottle of bourbon on weekends removes the acidic taste I get from drinking too much wine during the week.

Getting rid of the empties, though, is getting to be a real pain in the ass. To avoid the clinking of glass when sanitation picks up the garbage on Monday mornings, I now wrap the bottles in tissue paper, so they don't make too much noise.

My life is so screwed up, and my casual attitude toward God has now taken on a remorseful tone. Any prayer life I think about or intend to resume during the day gets erased at night by my drinking.

A few years too late, I begin to wonder if I might have made the wrong choice coming back to New York. My vague, ill-thought-out plan of reuniting my little family of three, didn't take into account that little boys grow up, turn into teenagers, and become their father's sons. Now, on the verge of graduating high school, busy with plans and friends, Brian and Brendan have their own ideas about life. At times, it feels like I'm not even part of their world, and that's when I drink more.

Passed out in a swivel chair, I fumble to recall last night's conversation with a potential real estate client, hoping I didn't come on to him or slur my words over the phone while attempting to get his house listing. I can't remember. Like my father, I've become a blackout drinker.

At times, I understand how my own choices have led me into this present hell. Other days, it feels good to blame my mother and her goddamn indifference and lack of support for all my problems. And then other times, I'm sure my ex-husband is the reason I'm living this fucked-up tragic life.

In this pitiful state of mind, I wonder why God is so hard on me, the one who went through so many dramatic life changes only to end up in the same place I tried to escape. When I ask, *Why God?* He remains silent, only adding to my frustration and emotional pain.

The Point of
No Return

B rian calls around nine o'clock on a Friday night in a panic. "Mom, something's wrong with Dad. He's sick and throwing up all over the place. I don't know what to do."

It's the kind of call I dreaded. Never having experienced withdrawals from alcohol, I have no idea what to expect when I arrive at the house. I see dismay and sadness sketched on Brian's face. Brendan looks distracted and angry. I kiss and hug them both, hoping to alleviate the morbid feel in the house.

Brian cocks his head toward the living room. I follow the blare of the television and notice a bucket filled with vomit near the couch. The room smells foul. Bill is huddled up on the sofa, shivering despite having a blanket over him. Drenched in sweat, he's shaking and talking nonsense.

"He doesn't want to go to the hospital," Brian whispers, hoping his father doesn't hear him.

Brian tells me his father has been detoxing since the night before and that his withdrawal symptoms seem to be getting worse. Looking down at my ex-husband, I feel a familiar rage well up in me for how goddamn selfish he is to let his sons see him in this condition.

How lucky he was to have a second chance and have his children back in his life. And this is what he does to show his love for them?

I feel the urge to pull him off the couch and slap him across the face for all the pain and upheaval he's caused us. Instead, I run into the bathroom to cry and hide my true feelings, but the nauseating smells of aftershave, shit, and vomit sends me back out.

I stay with the boys for the rest of the weekend, cleaning and making home-cooked meals. Being around them for this length of time feels right and brings back a happier time in Texas.

Over the weekend, I learn from Brian that his father hasn't paid the rent in two months, and the landlord is threatening eviction. He now pays $2800 a month plus utilities, and there's no honest way for me to come up with that kind of cash to loan him.

By late Saturday afternoon, Bill is standing up and taking small sips of ginger ale, but that's about it. He looks weak and unsteady on his feet. Staring at the cadaverous frame draped in boxer shorts, I shake my head in wonder, in what I saw in this man. The infatuation and wide-eyed wonder over his power and authority are long gone. He no longer has that mystical comforting hold over me, telling me everything is going to be okay when it's not. It never was. His drinking and lies made sure of that.

In between sips of ginger ale, he mumbles something about wanting to go to rehab.

"So you want to go to rehab because you're on the verge of being evicted, is that it?" I snap. "You want an escape hatch?"

He looks surprised that I know this bit of information and shoots Brian a look like my son's breached a trust for telling me something I wasn't supposed to know.

In this cryptic moment between father and son, I realize Bill is a negative role model to his children in more ways than his drinking.

I never quite mastered the art of approaching my mother in a calm, reasonable way, whatever that means. Her fixed, sour expression keeps me on the defensive, and I can never quite gauge what the hell is going on in her mind. This time I don't care. I'm direct and to the point.

"I need your help, Ma. Bill's having trouble paying the rent, and there's a strong possibility he's going to get evicted. I'm asking if the boys can stay here with us for a while. They can sleep in Timmy's old room."

"They'll do no such a thing!" she says, appalled at the request.

"Bill's drinking has gotten out of hand, and he needs to do a detox. He'll probably go into rehab after that. It'll only be for a month or two. The boys need a place to stay."

"That's not *my* problem," she snaps, crushing her cigarette into the ashtray.

"Yes, yes, it is your problem. These are your grandchildren," I say, determined to maintain my calm. "They have no other family but us to turn to."

"It most certainly is not my problem, and if you had listened to me years ago about marrying that guy, you wouldn't be in the mess that you're in today."

"Oh, you mean *that guy* you send cards to on his birthday and Father's Day?"

The verbal battle ends with a silent fume, and I retreat to the basement feeling angry and powerless. I pour myself a glass of wine, trying to calm the internal boil I'm all too familiar with when it comes to talking to her.

How could she say no? How could she deny her grandchildren a place to sleep when she's the only person in the world who can help? She had no problem giving my uncle a place to sleep when he needed it. What a heartless bitch! She doesn't give a shit about anyone but herself.

I rant on, talking to myself like this for a while, only to realize the liquor isn't working. I'm stone-cold sober when it registers with me that this woman, who calls herself a *mother*, is an enemy of mine. And maybe, always was. I knew she didn't care for me growing up, but I had no idea she would go to this length to hurt me or those I love. I'm stunned by my own dark revelation and wonder why I hadn't seen it before.

The thought of my sons forced to take care of their alcoholic father was bad enough, but now the looming threat of their homelessness sends me into a blind rage. Their father's irresponsible, drunken actions leave Brian and Brendan without options after graduation, much less give them any security before entering the real world.

In her refusal to take in her grandchildren when they need her the most, she betrays everything a mother is supposed to represent.

Does she hate me that much that she would deny her grandchildren a place to sleep?

This latest act of cruelty is the last straw awakening in me a tipping point of my own. Amid this searing insanity and pressure-cooker environment, I vow to act, to take control, to retaliate against all the injustice I've experienced with her. My mind reaches a watershed decision, and I cross a threshold I never dreamed I would or ever could.

———————

It's the pre-dawn age of Facebook and other social media outlets, but electronic banking has been around for a while. As a real estate agent, I have access to the local multiple listing services known as MLS.

And as of six months ago, I have access to my mother's savings account, which she put me on in case of an emergency. She doesn't use a computer and waits until the end of the month to get her bank statement in the mail. The bank has linked her account with mine electronically, and I can now see how much money she has in her savings account.

I surf the listings on MLS every night, hoping against hope to find something that the boys can live in and afford. The rental units are out of the question, but a small studio apartment, if purchased outright, would mean only paying the monthly maintenance, which runs anywhere from $150 to $300 a month. Even with a menial job, the boys can handle it. Once they settle into a place of their own, they can plan college or vocational school and move forward with their young lives.

For weeks I scour the different websites for possible locations taking into consideration the neighborhood, the condition of the building, the proximity to transportation, and of course, the price.

Bill has bought some time giving the landlord a few hundred bucks here and there, but it's only a matter of weeks before the landlord demands full payment. The clock is ticking.

Frantic with the vision of Brian and Brendan being homeless, two cheap studio listings miraculously appear. They're both in the same apartment complex, and both need work but require no board approval. With one click of the computer mouse, the cash from her bank account transfers into mine. Two weeks later, I close on the purchase of the two studio apartments. Before her bank statement gets mailed to the house, I will have depleted most of my mother's savings, giving her a valid reason to hate me.

WITHOUT A MAP

Meredith and her dog Buttons meet me at the door. Both have their own style of welcoming me. The poodle jumps up and licks my hand, and Meredith smiles warmly and shakes the other.

I've been seeing my therapist for the last eight months, and despite the vague dread I have walking into her office, I look forward to the visits. It's February, a nowhere month if you're not into Valentine's Day, and the only advantage for me is I'm ten days sober.

Today, in a lucid moment, I realize Meredith and her poodle have the same reddish curly brown hair. I laugh to myself, wondering how I hadn't noticed it before.

Without going into detail or mentioning its common in people who drink, Meredith referred me to a psychiatrist for depression. In my first and only visit, this overweight, bearded quack blatantly called me an alcoholic, a word Meredith never used in my presence. I told him to screw off, and if he must know, all I drink is wine. Just give me the prescription and keep your opinions to yourself, I tell him.

The nerve of that guy! He sees me once, talks to me for 15 minutes, and makes the snap judgment that I'm a drunk. What does he know about me or my life? If he had my life, he would drink too!

I grabbed the script out of his hand and ran from the office as fast as I could. The instructions on the bottle read: **Do not drink alcohol with this medication**. Hence the only reason I'm liquor-free for the last ten days. But honestly, I feel better already.

I'm beginning to trust Meredith. Trust is a big issue since I don't have any left for family, and whatever trust I placed in God has gotten swallowed up in a murky haze of alcohol, ambivalence, and guilt over the things I've done.

I'm a lost soul feeling the consequences of my actions, someone not prepared for any moral code ricocheting back on me for stealing. With all my notions about good and evil, it took a while to recognize the darkness in my own heart, a heart filled with hidden murderous rage, resentment, and bitterness over the path my life took. Sin is certainly a lot harder to identify in oneself than others.

Justifying my thievery, believing it could compensate for any gross emotional pain and lack of power I've experienced over the years, fell short of expectation. How could I have had the foresight to know my actions would lead to an overload of remorse and guilt? Now, detached from anything genuine within me, I've become my own stranger.

I rationalize that stealing Mother's money has an upside. The boys now have the stability of a place to call home, in a nice neighborhood, and a safe environment. They also have choices, although much harder ones than their friends who live at home with two parents. I tell myself that maybe this one action can save them from repeating harmful family patterns.

The idea of Bill entering rehab got nixed once the looming threat of three months overdue rent got resolved with his eviction. With no parental responsibilities, he now sleeps in the same office suite that he works out of during the day.

My actions have left Mother financially depleted, and we are now each other's prisoner, victims of our own doing. With one quick click of a mouse, I managed to strip away her last vestige of power. Making restitution will take a lot longer than a click.

Today, I plan on telling Meredith what I did. I don't know why. Maybe I'm seeking absolution from the one person I trust knowing she won't judge me as harshly as I'm judging myself.

In our last session, I asked her, "Do you think we're called upon to save others in this life?"

She wasn't surprised by the question. I guess there were plenty of other POWs sitting on her leather couch, stroking her poodle, asking that same question.

With a deep sigh, Meredith says that the only person we can save is our self. "We can't help another human being if we have the same affliction as the person we're trying to save. It's like trying to rescue a drowning man when you, yourself, don't know how to swim."

"What about spiritually saving them?" I whispered.

"Joan, I'm not the person to answer that question. But I guess my answer would be the same. The only person we can save in this life is our self."

I take in a deep breath and let out an equally deep groan. It wasn't the answer I wanted to hear. In truth, I didn't know how to save myself.

Before I can broach the subject of my absolution, Meredith announces that she won't be able to see me anymore. She's moving to Florida in the next few weeks to take care of her terminally ill brother and doesn't know if or when she will be returning.

Seeing the devastated look on my face, she places her hand on my shoulder and, in what will be our last and final session, gives me the gift of her professional understanding of my situation.

Meredith tells me my mother suffers from a severe form of Narcissistic Personality Disorder or NPD and that she's incapable of any real love or nurturing.

I say I've heard the term before, but I'm not really sure what it means.

She explains that narcissism is a recognized mental illness, an extreme form of self-centeredness characterized by a lack of empathy or feeling for others, that people with this disorder feel no guilt or remorse for their actions. They will manipulate, lie, use, and deceive others to get what they want.

"So, there's a name for people that don't give a shit about anyone but themselves?"

Meredith nods at my bluntness and continues. "Narcissists have an exaggerated sense of self-importance, and having a parent with this mental disorder creates a tremendous amount of stress and untold damage on the family, especially in children of the same sex. The level of genuine care and sacrifice required to raise a healthy child just doesn't happen in a narcissistic household. In healthy families, parents understand their inherent power and authority. They know their words have meaning, and their actions have consequences that will affect the child's well-being and development. These parents work hard to provide a healthy environment for the child to grow."

I was trying to follow her every word, struck by the implications of my upbringing.

"In unhealthy families, the focus is on the parents and fulfilling their needs. Chances are, your father knew something was wrong with your mother but didn't understand he was dealing with a narcissistic wife. By accepting her behavior as normal, his acquiescence gave your mother free rein to do and say whatever she wanted. As long as your father fulfilled his role as the breadwinner by bringing home the paycheck, your mother didn't question his problematic daily drinking. She had the power, and he was able to drink. It was a kind of trade-off for both of them, creating the kind of co-dependent homeostasis needed to keep their marriage going. I see it in many families. It contributes greatly to creating the same dysfunctional patterns in the next generation."

I stare at her.

"Your religion played a vital role in the family dynamics as well, Joan. Your mother's most powerful tool to control her children was using the 'honor thy mother' mantra to justify her wanton neglect and verbal abuse. She got her sense of maternal omnipotence by proclaiming to have God on her side. And as you know, it's impossible to argue with God, especially the one who punishes little children for disobedience."

My head spins, trying to comprehend what she's saying. I'm not sure how to respond. I'm not even sure I like what's coming out of her mouth right now, so I just weakly smile back.

"No one in your family came out of this unscathed, Joan. Not even the fair-haired Timmy. Despite what you believe, your mother's affection for your brother held all kinds of mixed, subliminal messages that lacked any healthy maternal boundaries. She gave him the time and attention you and your sister never received, but Timmy paid a high price for engaging in the role of what we call the 'golden child.' And, from what you said, he also played the role of the family 'mascot' deflecting whatever tension he sensed in the family with humor. Let me guess; your mother protected him from taking responsibility for any of his actions, and he could do no wrong?"

How does she know that?

"It's all part of the syndrome of being engulfed in the web of a narcissistic mother. I'm sure your mother tried to sabotage his relationships with women over the years, making little off-handed, sarcastic comments about his girlfriends, giving Timmy the impression that no woman was good enough for him."

I nod my head in agreement, still surprised she knows all this.

"Timmy lives with these subliminal sexual messages that your mother should be the only woman in his life. After your father died, she wanted Timmy to become an extension of her husband."

No wonder he never comes around to visit her.

"It's no surprise that Timmy is childless and on his third marriage. What your mother did to him is called 'covert' or 'emotional' incest."

"Yeah, so creepy," is all I can manage to say.

"My dear, everything you've told me about your life and struggles, how you feel about things, all points to being born into a narcissistic and alcoholic family. It's a family system that is extremely difficult, if not impossible, to disengage from. It sets everyone up to fail in one way or another. A father's role is to love and protect his daughter. Your father couldn't do either of those two things, because his purpose in the marriage, outside of being the breadwinner, was to keep your mother happy. The mental health community calls it 'orbiting,' which is when one spouse revolves their world around the other to keep the marriage in place."

"He was more like a spinning top around her," I joke, trying to ease the tension I feel.

"It's understandable why you feel victimized by your father, but I don't believe his molestation of you was intentional, Joan. His alcoholic blackouts triggered some unmet physical needs that weren't being satisfied in the marriage. By all accounts, your dad was a good man who tried hard to live up to the duties of being the traditional father and husband, but he *was* an alcoholic. He probably suffered from clinical depression as well, and drinking was how he coped with the stresses of his life and marriage."

Buttons stares up at me with his watery brown eyes. His cold, wet snout snuggles against my thigh as though he senses my distress and sadness. The animal's empathy is comforting, and I stroke the poodle acknowledging his love. Meredith passes me the box of tissues on the table and adjusts her glasses, giving me a chance to breathe.

I shake my head in disbelief. "I'm so confused by that term, alcoholic," I say. "How could my father be one? He went to work every day and never called in sick from a hangover. Even though he drove drunk at times, he never got a DUI for it. He never went to bars; he always drank at home. I know he never cheated on my mother or gambled away his paycheck. He handed it to her on Fridays. I saw him do it. How could he be an alcoholic? Real ones drink from brown paper bags and don't have jobs."

Meredith gives me a questioning look. She reminds me that the criteria for being an alcoholic include daily drinking, drinking alone, and having frequent blackouts.

"Your father's sexual abuse during one of his blackouts and your mother's mental illness had a crippling effect on Cathleen's development," she noted. "It happened at the age of 13, a critical time when a young girl's sexual identity is just beginning to form. Cathleen's acting out with older men was a cry for help that went unheeded. When her teenage troubles started, your parents didn't know how to cope with her bad-girl behavior. Your mother was probably deeply ashamed. She could only see your sister as a reflection of herself. Her narcissistic mirror rejected what she saw as Cathy's unacceptable behavior. Instead of trying to help and understand her daughter, your mother no longer saw anything in her to love.

This pattern of my mother's behavior certainly made sense.

"Joan, your parents couldn't deal with conflict. They didn't know how to communicate and express their feelings on any meaningful level between themselves or their children. From all accounts, the only way they could communicate was to blame each other or pretend something didn't exist.

"They didn't take responsibility for their actions either, Meredith. It was as though my and Cathy's acting out had nothing to do with what was going on in the family," I say.

Meredith nods in recognition. "Your sister's way of coping with her early trauma, to escape the shame, was to move away. Ironically, that move to Texas validated your mother's assessment of Cathleen as the bad girl who didn't want to obey the rules, allowing everyone to believe she was the cause for the fracture in the family. Making Cathleen the family 'scapegoat,' allowed your parents to feel less guilty about the move to their new house on City Island."

With all these disturbing revelations, I'm ready to crawl out of my skin. "And what's my goddamn label?"

It was a question that came out more angry and sarcastic than intended. I give Meredith an apologetic look and ask in a hoarse whisper, "Is this what our lives get reduced to, a diagnostic label? It feels so goddamn cold."

Without waiting for an answer, I ask if we can take a break. Meredith obliges, directing me down the hall toward the bathroom. The splash of cold water feels good against my face. I barely recognize the person looking back in the mirror. I sit on the toilet, waiting for my hands to stop shaking.

What the hell just happened in there? I feel like I've been flayed alive. Was it all one big lie, one giant clusterfuck?

When I return to the couch, Buttons finds his place back on my thigh. Meredith asks if I'm okay. She leans back in her chair and offers me a bottle of water, giving me time to digest her previous words. She waits on me to continue.

"Is this mental disorder, this narcissism something my mother was born with or is it something that just happened to her?"

"The mental health community recognizes narcissism as a legitimate personality disorder but seem divided by its origins or how to treat it. Is it nurture or nature? It could be genetic. Some people are hardwired, predisposed toward it, but the environment plays a significant factor as well. If a child is abused or neglected while growing up, it could lead to a form of narcissism. But even the opposite, excessive pampering by parents, can give a child an overinflated sense of self."

I nod even though I'm thoroughly confused by her explanation.

"It's a complex disorder to study because there are degrees of narcissism in almost everyone and the ones who are the most damaged, who are the most toxic -- well let's just say, I don't see many of them coming through my office. Most times, it's their victims that seek my help. Diagnostically, narcissism is considered a gross distortion of a person's true self with fear and low self-esteem as the main underlying characteristics. A narcissistic person can't resolve their sense of inferiority they see in themselves, so they present an inflated image of themselves to the world."

Sobbing, I try to share my thoughts. "I knew my mother didn't love me, and at some point, I knew she didn't like me either. In her mind, I was this tragic loser, someone who could only get a married man to love me, and certainly not smart enough to get a college degree or be a managing editor of a newspaper. You know, she never asked about my experiences in Texas or that part of my life."

"I'm not surprised," said Meredith. "People like your mother don't like to feel threatened, and you threatened her with your confidence and courage in your ability to do things."

"I think I always knew something was wrong with her and prayed to God never to get what she had. Maybe that's why my father thought I didn't love her. I don't know, there was always something in me that wanted, needed to love and be loved by her, but it just never happened. It was too hard."

Realizing I'm talking about my mother in the past tense, I crumble into sobs so violent I lose my breath.

Meredith takes my hand and whispers quietly, "For all the suffering you've endured, you're the lucky one, Joan. You sought help outside the family system. And your birth order may have dictated a less damaging role than the rest of your siblings."

"Ah, now let me guess my diagnostic label, the family loser?"

"No. You were what the psychiatric world calls the 'lost or invisible' child, the middle daughter who was rarely seen or heard from in the family. You were the one who kept your head down, didn't make waves, or create any problems growing up. You took the wait and see stance, maintaining the status quo by not making any emotional demands upon your parents. Except, of course, when you broke out of that role and confronted your father as an adult."

I think of the inner voice that spoke to me so long ago and wondered if that was God's plan all along. Had it not been for that voice, I could have stayed a lost soul forever.

"It was all so hard," was all I could say.

"God blessed you with an active and curious imagination as a child, Joan, one that enabled you to play outside the home for long stretches at a time. And when forced to live prematurely on your own as a young woman, you learned to educate yourself through reading and writing, living with dreams of one day becoming a writer. I believe it was C. S Lewis, who once said, 'We read to know we're not alone.' And you, my dear child, are not alone."

I smile at her depiction of me.

"Dreaming and fantasizing may seem like random activities, but they're also survival skills that helped you cope with the emotional abandonment and neglect by your family. You're an extremely self-reliant individual, and this trait proved critical in the monumental task of moving out of New York with two young children. It took plenty of strength, stamina, and courage to do what you did, re-establishing yourself in an unfamiliar environment, getting a degree and becoming a successful journalist in a community that recognized your value."

I'm taken aback by her kind words and insights. No one in my family ever recognized my accomplishments or talents. And I never saw myself as strong or even self-reliant. I just always did what I had to do. Taking small sips of water, I sit quietly, reflecting on Meredith's words, finally touching on my father and his silence toward me in the last 18 months of his life.

"All he had to do was say he was sorry."

Meredith gives me a quizzical look.

"My father. All he had to do was apologize, and it could have been over. How can I still love my father after what he did, or didn't do? Why did he have to die without saying he was sorry, or even that he loved me? But I still love him, and it's an ache that doesn't go away."

Meredith nods her head. "One indiscretion doesn't negate the relationship we have with our parents. You may have loved him more than he loved you, but that's okay. You loved, that's the important thing. Like a parent who favors one child over another, kids do the same with parents. Children bond with the parent they relate to the most, even if that parent's behavior is harmful. Your mother bonded with her father, who, by the sound of it, was also narcissistic, and she had very little good to say about your grandmother, who you thought was a kind, lovely woman. We bond with those whose qualities are similar to ours.

It's clear your mother doesn't relate to other women. Whatever the reason, her aberrant behavior is no excuse for the way she treated her daughters, and still does. But ask yourself, Joan, how can a mother have no love or empathy for her daughters without there being some form of self-hate?"

I nod. "Yeah, I know what you're saying, but it doesn't help in understanding her. I always thought she was weird because of my grandfather, who got all feely-touchy with Cathy and me, that he might have done the same thing to her. Why the hell would she want to be like him?"

"Maybe she was attracted to his power," Meredith suggests. "From what you say, he was an imposing authority figure. But I suspect that your mother lives with a deep sense of shame. All narcissists have it. It's their real identity. It's the kind of deep-seated, internalized emotion that says you're not good enough as a human being, as a person worthy of love and success. Narcissistic personalities like to project that shame onto others. It's what your mother did to you."

"I know what you mean," I say. "I've lived with feeling less than all my life. Sometimes, I think I married my mother, too. She and Bill are so much alike. When you stop putting their needs first, stop trying to please them, stop listening to them because they never listen back; that's when they turn on you, making you feel you've done absolutely nothing for them. I thought Bill and my mother were just selfish, but now I see it's more than that. They make you feel worthless, and whatever you've done for them in the past means nothing. It was the same pattern before and during my marriage."

"Let me tell you something, Joan. You have a strong, resilient character that didn't completely buy into your family's depiction of you as a loser. But, like it or not, we do marry both our parents. Your marriage was an extension of your relationship with your father *and* mother. The two men were very similar. In the beginning, at least, your husband gave you the attention and protection that your father couldn't. But it's your mother and Bill who are emotionally similar and share many of the same narcissistic traits."

"Oh yeah," I nod in agreement.

"Bill's inability to get sober began the unraveling of your marriage. Even before you learned the extent of his lies, he started to shut you down, which understandably you took as rejection. He didn't want you to know about his false self, and his only defense was to ignore you. Your mother did the same thing by throwing you out after confronting your father. In the end, Bill and your mother weren't interested in the truth or their family's wellbeing. They were only interested in keeping up their false facades – Bill as the soldier hero and your mother living the illusion of being in a perfect marriage."

I just sat there stunned by her words. Everything she said I knew was the truth, but saying it out loud, felt like a sledgehammer splitting my head in two.

"Speaking up for yourself upset their narcissistic way of life, Joan. That's why they shut you down. Their egocentric actions brought you here and a few steps closer to being free. Nothing goes to waste in the universe. You will heal from this, Joan. You're a beautiful soul with an indomitable spirit and an inner strength that can tackle anything life has to throw at you, including that drinking problem of yours. I do hope you seek help for it," she said with all sincerity.

Standing at the doorway, after much hesitation, Meredith and I hug. I wished her good luck in Florida and thanked her for her service. I bent down and stroked her poodle one last time. As the door closed behind me, I couldn't help but think, *now what am I going to do?*

FINDING ANOTHER WAY

T he small church basement fills up with an odd assort-
ment of men and women, young and old, mostly old.
Some of them look dirty and disheveled, and others appear
a bit psycho. Except for me, everyone in the room is smiling.
They all seem to be happy sitting in this cramped, musty
space.

The basement is in the same church we held my father's
funeral so long ago. Today's his birthday. And, in the spirit
of trying to find meaning in my shattered fucked-up world,
I have declared today as my official sober date.

Tonight, I'm back in reporter mode. I'm the one carrying
a pad and pencil prepared to tell people I'm writing an article
for the local newspaper if they ask.

A man with an oversized belly and coffee stains on his
pink Izod polo smiles at me. He's sitting near the door, holding a half-smoked unlit stogy smelling like cigar smoke.

"I'm Big Richie," he says with a smile.

Of course, you are.

I give him an obligatory smile.

"You're new, welcome."

I want to protest, tell him I'm a reporter, but before I can explain, he points to the table where a 100-cup coffee pot sits. I grab a Styrofoam cup laying among the empty packets of sugar and wooden stirrers scattered across the table. I pour what's left in the pot, but it's clear I'm getting the dregs. I'm not impressed by all this messiness. I'm doubly annoyed at listening to this Richie guy order me around only to get a shitty cup of coffee.

Not a good start.

I find an empty seat on one of the few remaining folding chairs available. The meeting is supposed to start at 8 o'clock, and just as I look toward the clock, I hear someone say, "Good evening, my name is Tommy, and I'm an alcoholic."

The lady sitting next to me welcomes me and tells me it's an open meeting.

"My name is Maureen," she whispers.

Her dewy brown eyes show kindness, and she smiles easily.

Well, I didn't have to buy a ticket, so I guess that's why they call it an open meeting. I write the words 'open meeting' on my pad. I will write down everything I hear tonight. It will give me something to do during the hour. And if they talk fast, I can use my old Gregg steno skills.

My mind holds ambivalent thoughts at being in an Alcoholics Anonymous meeting. I'm vaguely aware I belong here. But it doesn't stop the voices screaming in my head to run the hell out before it's too late. I'm overwhelmed by these conflicting thoughts. I think I'm an alcoholic, but I hate the sound of the word. Maybe if there was another term for it, I could accept this new questionable identity.

I recently took a quiz from an old 'Dear Abby' newspaper column and answered more yes than no to questions about being an alcoholic. According to the results, I am, but what the hell does Abby know?

I keep asking myself over and over: how can I be an alcoholic? I have two jobs. I own a car. I've never gotten pulled over or arrested for drunk driving, or none of the other red flags that come with this disease. In looking around the room, it's sure to be the case with most of these people.

I feel lost in every sense of the word. The irony doesn't escape me that I'm sitting in an AA meeting while my ex-husband lives in an office building, painting little toy soldiers and drinking rum and coke from a coffee mug.

How the hell did I get here?

Surely a bottle or two of wine some nights doesn't make an alcoholic. But what about the compulsive desire to drink, or experiencing those unpredictable blackouts that Meredith and I discussed? I can't argue that I drank myself into isolation over the last several years, drinking in my mother's basement and talking to the same computer screen I did back in Texas five years ago.

Now that I feel the kids are safe in their apartments, I have a bit of clarity about my problems. But the idea of adding alcoholic to an already shaky identity compounds the shame I feel about myself.

Tonight is not my first AA meeting. I tried one or two in Connecticut after work, believing that it has a better class of drunk other than here in the Bronx; another theory of mine that got shot in the ass under closer scrutiny.

At one of those meetings, a nice woman by the name of Grace G. asked if I needed a sponsor, and I said, "I guess so." This same nice woman suddenly turned into a female prison guard, telling me I needed to get a copy of 'The Big Book,' start working the 12 Steps, and then she demanded I go to a meeting every night. That was the end of Grace and me. I wasn't ready for that kind of sponsorship. Maybe that's how it ended with Bill and the guy who sponsored him, though I'll never know.

There's nothing heroic about my decision to enter AA. It's a last-ditch effort on my part after losing Meredith as my therapist. I don't have the energy to try to find another sympathetic mother figure. Rehab is out. I'd never subject myself to the humiliation of telling my employer I have a drinking problem over a bottle of wine.

This idea of going to meetings to get sober seems palpable. I certainly can do it for 90 days, which appears to be the magic number everyone throws out. I can do 90 meetings in 90 days. Then I'll be fine.

The woman next to me is smiling up at that guy Tommy still talking at the podium. I don't know what she finds so amusing because what I'm hearing sounds rather sad and pathetic. I write down 'sad and pathetic' in steno, so she can't read it. Tommy is a 50-year-old biker who started drinking at the age of nine.

Oh please, nothing here I can relate to, I was praying the rosary at the age of nine!

I look around the room and see that most of this bunch is male, which adds another thread of humiliation sewn into my blanket of shame.

Women aren't supposed to be alcoholics.

The thought shakes me to the core, and I want to bolt out the door. I feel Maureen's hand on my knee calming me down, as though she just read my thoughts. Never taking her eyes off the guy at the podium and still smiling, she keeps me in my seat for the rest of the meeting.

I hear the words liar and thief in the biker's story and know somehow those same words pertain to me. But for now, rationalization will have its way, keeping me from admitting they are as much a part of my new identity as the word alcoholic.

The meeting ends with the Lord's Prayer, and I throw the pad and pencil back into my bag, ready to run. Maureen gently takes my hand, and I give my second obligatory smile for the night.

God, what does she want?

People linger afterward, talking effortlessly with each other, putting away chairs, laughing, joking about God-knows-what. I don't know what the hell is so wonderful about all this.

Maureen asks my name. I hesitate, not sure I want to tell her. Why waste time if I'm not coming back? But there's something about her demeanor, a serenity that defies my hesitation, so I tell her.

"You know, Joan, we are all a little 'sad and pathetic' when we first come into the rooms of AA. This disease wants to destroy us if we let it. I think you're in the right place."

My cheeks flush at the sound of my own words coming out of her mouth.

She laughs at the dumbstruck look on my face and tells me her steno skills are pretty rusty, but she still knows how to read shorthand. It's the first genuine smile I give all night.

This woman's easygoing demeanor and her eyes radiating genuine kindness will be the seed that keeps me in the rooms of AA. After all, I can do anything for 90 days, and then I'll be on my way.

As the nights sitting in AA meetings turn into weeks, I begin to form clarity, slowly seeing myself through an objective lens. But the emotional suffering in almost every thought I have through that same lens propels me back to the idea of drinking.

With each new day in recovery, I still long for that one glass of merlot. Some days, I can actually smell and taste the wine going down. Sometimes, in my sleep, I dream I'm drinking and wake up in a cold sweat. My compulsive thoughts fight for dominance, telling me that all I need, all I want, is just one glass of the dark elixir.

Every day, I have to white-knuckle it until a lucid moment of grace steps in allowing me to concede I never really knew how to drink safely without it turning into a bottle or two.

It's a daily mental battle grieving the loss of pleasure and comfort that alcohol gave me. It was the only vehicle that let me drive away with abandonment all the negative thoughts I have about myself, my life, and my family. Drinking seemed like the answer to all my pain, but in the end, even it betrayed me. All I have left is me -- a divorced middle-aged woman estranged from herself and the world she knew. Now that's sad and pathetic!

I hear and read the AA slogans like "One day at a time," "Easy does it," "To thine own self be true." But the urge to romanticize how much fun it was to drink becomes more volatile after gaining a little sober time. I'm at a mental crossroads and find myself randomly thinking, *Hey, this isn't so bad. I was able to stay sober for 90 days. I can drink and come back in again. If I did 90 days, I could certainly do it again.*

This kind of thinking makes me believe I'm still in control, an idea my sponsor quickly dismisses. Yet, the urge to drink is always lurking in the back of my mind.

Just one glass of wine to relax, that's all I want.

At meetings, I hear someone say, "I came for my drinking, but stayed for my thinking," or, "It's the first drink that gets you drunk." It's not the catchy slogans that keep me from acting on impulse. It's the reality of seeing what happens to those who do, the men and women who play a game with their life believing they can go out drinking and drugging one more time, but never come back. Sad as it is to say out loud, it's in another person's tragedy that I find the strength to stay sober and accept the wisdom of the program.

I begin to identify my grief for the loss of alcohol in terms of Elizabeth Kubler-Ross's five stages of grief over death – denial, anger, bargaining, depression, and acceptance. I denied I had a problem. I'm angry at everything, and everyone who I believe gave me this problem. I bargain with the idea of having 'just one' glass of wine. Depression sets in at the thought of never being able to drink again. And then ever so gradually, accepting the idea of living a sober lifestyle. All these stages will take years to process, understand, and live. For the moment, my only job is to stay sober one day, sometimes one minute at a time.

"Don't drink and go to meetings," is the mantra that gets me through my first year.

It's May 6, 2006. I'm celebrating my first year sober in the same small, musty church basement I entered a year ago. Memories of my father still linger, and I wonder if he were still alive, would he be joining the ranks of AA. Would he be proud of me for doing so, or would he even care? Would my father understand today, what I was trying to do that fateful day in the kitchen in 1990? That I just wanted to heal. I wanted it for all of us. These are the questions with no answers. The emotional landmines and triggers that could lead me back to the bottle.

Unlike that day in the kitchen, today, I've come to understand that some people don't want to recover or heal from their addictions and inner wounds. The cost is too high. If my father admitted any wrongdoing, he would also have to admit he had a problem with alcohol.

I arrive at my first anniversary by going to several meetings a week, following the advice of old-timers, those who know a thing or two about sobriety; the men and women who say that all genuine recovery begins once the obsession to drink lifts.

This obsession, which some also call compulsion, is a strange animal and different for everyone. For some, the fixation on drinking never ends; for others, it can be 30 to 60 days. For me, it was a long 90 days.

In reading the AA literature, I came to understand that only when the body is free from the obsession of alcohol, can the mind and spirit begin a renewal process, a kind of 'out with the old and in with the new' thought transformation. The old-timers emphasize that all emotional healing is a journey, not a destination, and if that's true, I'm traveling at a snail's pace.

The room fills up with friends and strangers. No one in my family shows up to celebrate this momentous occasion. Everyone drinks, so coming to my anniversary would make them uncomfortable. My children seemed shocked that I even identify as an alcoholic, so they find reasons not to attend. I wonder how different my life would be if Bill remained in AA during our marriage, worked his program, and got honest with himself as a person.

Would we still be together? Would my children be more open to the idea that alcoholism is a family disease?

I've heard several men tell their story, guys who, for one reason or another, remind me of Bill, leaving me to wonder what makes a person choose recovery and another reject it? There are no easy answers, but without exception, the men with long-term sobriety mention getting honest and becoming teachable as the two key factors. Some say the only place they were able to become truthful was in the company of other alcoholics, which, in turn, helped them to find their higher power.

This last year has been tough, and I learned first-hand how difficult it is to stop drinking. I have more compassion toward those who suffer from this disease. In recovery, everything has to change; the people, the places, the things, even the attitude toward change. Learning how to live sober is the hardest thing I've had to do.

I'm still living in my mother's basement, but that arrangement no longer justifies my drinking. I want sobriety, and am willing to learn a new way of life without the crutch of a drink. I have the necessary tools to help me succeed: don't drink, go to meetings, get a home group, get a sponsor, and get active in AA.

For now, my world has narrowed significantly. I go to work and meetings. I make coffee and bring cookies to my homegroup on Tuesday night, and I help clean up afterward. I stay close to my sponsor, who I'm beginning to trust. I'm even starting to smile.

At 51 years old, I'm learning to navigate a new world without a drink. The daily challenges of life are always there, the internal ones too. Admittedly, I'm thick-headed and willful, traits that block my path and delay my progress. Like most, I'm sensitive to my surroundings, and the stress of being around people who bullshit and lie can be emotionally overwhelming. "Live and let live" has become an essential part of my spiritual journey.

The core of AA is working the 12 Steps. At times, I regret pushing God out of my life. Maybe if I had known about the family dynamics earlier, it would have been different. Then again, maybe Meredith and AA was part of His plan all along, helping me to understand my family history, so I don't repeat it. I can move forward. Sobriety is part of my spiritual maturity, deepening my reliance on God and the unseen forces.

I see people in the rooms struggling to find who and what their higher power is, and I want to shout, "God is real! I know He exists. I met Him in the wind! That last remark wouldn't go over too well with this group of pragmatic skeptics.

Besides, who am I to preach to another suffering soul? It's a personal journey that everyone must choose for themselves. What right do I have telling another stubborn alcoholic the means to find their joy or what road to take? My spiritual path wasn't a straight run. It had a lot of twists and turns. Maybe that's how life is, a process of uncovering its mystery.

Step 3 encourages us to turn our will and life over to the care of God as we understand Him. Today, I know that God doesn't punish. He doesn't destroy us for our sins. We do that quite nicely on our own. It took the fellowship of Alcoholics Anonymous and breaking down emotionally to come to a new understanding of Him. For that, I am grateful.

The floor fans quiver, spewing out hot air around the room. Men and women begin to fill the tight rows of folding chairs in the small, musty basement. Over the past year, I attended a lot of meetings in the Bronx and lower Westchester, and tonight many of the people I met are here to help me celebrate.

Looking over at the melted layer cake with my name on it, and the pile of cards and gifts waiting for me, I'm overwhelmed by the love I feel in this room. Everyone is smiling and joking. And today, unlike a year ago, I understand what that means. Joy and happiness are the offshoots of sobriety. When one of us makes their first year, everyone celebrates. These recovering alcoholics know the struggle and pain it takes to get here.

Sitting in the front row is Maureen looking up at the podium and smiling at me like a proud mama. She hands me a long-stemmed dark pink rose, the color symbolizing gratitude. It's a reminder of what she believes sobriety represents: the opportunity to begin anew and become the person God meant us to be.

Standing at the podium, this elongated view of the room is intimidating. All I see are hot, sweaty faces smiling back at me. I want to cry at the beauty of this moment. I'm overwhelmed by all the attention and feel tempted to run out the door. I laugh, knowing nothing about me has changed, yet everything has. I search for the familiar faces of Tommy the Biker, and Big Richie sitting in their usual place. They smile. I'm ready.

"Good evening, my name is Joan, and I'm an alcoholic."

A FRESH START

The phone rings. It's 6:30 in the morning.

Who could be calling this early? Who has my new phone number? It's probably a telemarketer.

"Hello?"

"It's your mother. I need you to take me to the hospital."

Suddenly I remember the only person who has my new number. Mother announces it's her like I don't recognize that scratchy, jarring tone after all these years.

Sometimes when I call her, she asks, "Who's this?"

I tell her a stranger, which isn't far from the truth.

"There's something wrong with me. I don't feel well. I need you to take me to the hospital today, right now."

Doesn't she remember this is a big day for me? I distinctly remember telling her that today was the grand opening for the new apartment complex located on the Hudson River, the 300-unit luxury building that I will be managing.

I feel that old familiar anger rising in me, wondering if she's setting me up to fail again. I take a deep breath and repeat the prayer that has gotten me thus far.

God grant me the serenity to accept the things I cannot change, the courage to change the things I can, and the wisdom to know the difference.

"Are you there?"

"What's wrong, Ma?"

"I have terrible pain in my stomach, and blood is coming out of my stools."

I groan inwardly. "What about Timmy? Can't he drive you? You know I have the grand opening today."

"Joanie, you know I wouldn't bother you if I didn't think it was serious and needed medical attention."

A few months after celebrating my first year sober, I got the opportunity to train as a property manager, and with the new position came a rent-free apartment.

God is good!

I jumped at the chance to move out of the basement and into a spacious one-bedroom apartment overlooking the river.

My new salary takes care of Ma's bills and expenses, as well as slowly paying back the money I stole from her savings account. The move from the basement comes with plenty of survivor's guilt, a form of PTSD associated with long-term family trauma, a disorder I'm only beginning to process and understand.

I weigh my suspicious nature of her ulterior motives against the indisputable concern in her voice and tell her I will need to clear it with my boss before I can do anything. The cynic in me is still alive. If it were me and the roles were reversed, she'd tell me to suck it up.

I feel a familiar pang of guilt when she opens the front door. It's evident from the way she's holding her stomach that she's in real pain. I grab her coat and purse, and off we go to the emergency room in New Rochelle.

After waiting hours for the test results, the doctor diagnoses it as a perforated colon, a condition that would need immediate care and perhaps an operation. The intake specialist asks her questions about her health, and the kind of medication, if any, she takes. When he asks if she smokes, Mother looks at him like he's a loon and shakes her head.

I find her lack of disclosure laughable. For years, her two-pack-a-day smoking habit has played havoc on her lungs, causing early emphysema and requiring the use of an inhaler. She's very fortunate her condition didn't worsen into carrying around an oxygen tank.

"My lungs have nothing to do with my colon," she says.

I'm concerned more about her having to undergo an operation while withdrawing from nicotine. It could severely weaken her immune system causing complications, and I tell her so.

Later the doctor confides that he will be doing a laparoscopic procedure to reduce any risk caused by her age. When I tell her the good news, she gives me a smirk that says, "See, I told you so."

Mother's acute anxiety and sudden panic attacks over the years were treated as usual by my father and viewed as hypochondria by her children. She used her symptoms as a reason to justify why she didn't work or drive but did nothing to remedy her condition over the years. She would freak out at the slightest change to her daily routine, but now, under the current circumstances, her anxiety is justified.

A few weeks shy of her 80th birthday, and except for childbirth, today is her first stay in a hospital. As I watch the medical staff put an IV of antibiotics and pain medication into her arm, the fear on her face is palpable.

I tell her not to worry that she's in a safe place with a staff of professionals. I let her know I'll be at the hospital every day, keeping an eye on what the doctor and staff are doing. I make this promise knowing full well the timing of all these new events is rattling in me like a loose screw inside a cylinder. My mind fast-forwards to the possibility of her dying.

Don't be silly. It's just a colon.

The thought stays with me, and I push it further than I should for someone new in sobriety. Mother's hospitalization could be the beginning of long-term care, and at 80, that's not a stretch. It could also mean a time when things get sorted out between us.

At this point in my musings, I have to tell myself how ridiculous I sound for thinking such a thing. Reconciliation between my narcissistic mother and me is part of that distorted family image that got me into trouble in the first place. Wanting a simple apology from my father that never materialized, of wanting closure that never happened either. I can hear her now.

What do I have to apologize for? I didn't do anything to you! If anything, you need to say you're sorry to me for what you did.

Sobriety helps to entertain all these scenarios without wanting a drink. Processing these painful, sometimes difficult emotions takes time, and I don't want to dwell on something that hasn't happened yet.

"Reason over emotion" is a slogan I find helpful. I keep a journal to record my feelings and things I'm grateful for, even the smallest of things. This list includes the big stuff like a new job and a free apartment but also the opportunity to call upon God to guide me through these stressful times.

My mother successfully undergoes the laparoscopic procedure for her perforated colon, but a few days later, she contracts a staph infection resistant to antibiotics. She's put into isolation, a sterile room with only a glass window for her to stare out and scowl at the nursing staff. To enter her room, I have to wear medical overalls, a mask, and gloves.

Seeing her in this self-contained room freaks me out, but I'm thankful to the nurse who says I can only stay 10 minutes. Ma looks vulnerable, like a caged feral animal, complaining about everything from the food to the staff, to what's not on television.

She's five days without a cigarette, and I attribute her current frame of mind from nicotine withdrawal, but she'll never admit that's the reason. Instead, she verbally rips through everything and everyone in the hospital, including me, saying I look like I want to leave.

"You think I like being in this hazmat suit and wearing rubber gloves?" I say, handing her a glass of water.

I talk about my new job, and she tells me she has constipation. I silence my exasperation with the mantra: *this too shall pass.*

"The good news is the doctors say once the infection clears in seven to 10 days, you'll be able to go home."

"I don't want to go home."

"What do you mean?"

"I don't want to climb those stairs anymore."

"Well, let's cross that bridge when we get to it."

"No, no, no. I don't want to go home." She repeats herself like a petulant child.

"Ma, what are you saying, that you want to go into a nursing home?" I'm secretly hoping she doesn't want to live with me in the new apartment.

"If I have to," she pouts.

I'm stunned. The house on City Island has always been my mother's protective womb, her security blanket, and the center of her power. Not wanting to return to the only place she's known since 1972 shocks me. I don't know what to make of this sudden announcement but said I'd look into alternatives with the hospital staff.

Over the next few weeks, as she recuperates in isolation, I meet with the hospital social worker and staff to see what options we have. Mother mentions going to the same nursing home as her parents, but unless we can pay out of pocket, the family has to settle for what Medicare covers and what facility has a bed available at the time of discharge. It turns out, her medical insurance covers only a certain number of days in the hospital, and the hospital is transporting her to a rehabilitation facility. The rehab is a local nursing home, so she'll get to test out the facilities before she decides if she wants to move there permanently.

The pungent odor of urine and old age reminds me of those Sunday visits to see my grandparents. A few weeks into her nursing home stay, Ma falls and fractures her hip, causing a blood clot in her left leg. This incident sends her back to the hospital. The constant shifting between the hospital and the nursing home over the last month has taken its toll, and her health is visibly deteriorating. She has frequent low-grade fevers and is not eating. Her complaints about hospital food are legitimate, so I bring her a variety of foods and desserts on my nightly visits.

The doctors have her on a blood thinner for the clot in her leg, pain medication for the fractured hip, and her hands are black and blue from the constant change in catheters. Under these circumstances, she has the right to be testy, so I brace myself for our daily visit, but unbeknownst to me, the doctors have also put her on an anti-depressant.

I enter the hospital room one weekend to find a stranger sitting in a wheelchair. This senior citizen *looks* like my mother with the same over-permed grey curly hair and wrinkly face, but her demeanor is soft and gentle. She looks up and greets me with a smile.

"I'm sorry," I say. "Do I have the wrong room?"

A raised highbrow reminds me it's her.

"I brought you some pot roast with gravy for tonight and turkey on rye with pickles for lunch. The doctors tell me you're not eating. You need to eat something, Ma."

"I don't have an appetite. Did you bring any cigarettes?"

Her tone carries none of the general irritability or annoyance that my presence usually brings out in her. It's more neutral, almost peaceful.

I hold her hand and feel the frailness of her failing body. It takes a moment to soak up this new human being, one nearing the end of her days but has somehow transformed into a nice, calm, and dare I say, happy mother -- all from a little blue pill.

I wheel her out of the hospital room and into the corridor. While waiting for the elevator, she greets the nurses at the station with an unprecedented smile and tells them she is going to the outdoor area for a cigarette.

"Oh, by the way," she says, "Did you meet my daughter, Joan?"

I marvel at this new life form, one who can hold a simple conversation with others without first pissing them off.

God, if only she took those anti-depressant pills 40 years ago.

The sliding glass doors open into an enclosed outdoor garden, a section of the hospital filled with the aromatic fragrance of gardenias and calendulas. It's a welcome change from the stench of sickness and bowel movements just a few steps away.

It's September, and the temperature is a comfortable 75 degrees. The mild heat seems to increase the fragrance of the flowers. The surrounding potted palm trees add to the pleasant ambiance of this therapeutic oasis, shading us from the mid-morning sun.

Mother lights up one of her long-awaited cigarettes, inhaling it like oxygen. In this park-like setting, I sit on a small red bench directly facing her in the wheelchair and unpack the turkey sandwiches preparing us for lunch. I begin peeling the rind off a tangerine, hoping the tangy fragrance will stimulate her appetite.

I'm not my usual guarded self and feel a beautiful peacefulness between us defying past encounters. Ma's eyes reflect none of the irritation I'm accustomed to, and her smile toward me is genuine. I feel encouraged by this new countenance.

"Life's hard right now, Ma. This new job is kicking my ass. I'm dealing with 20 employees, and everyone's got an issue. The maintenance guy is complaining someone stole his mop and bucket, and that's why he can't clean the compactor rooms over the weekend. Another one said her boyfriend borrowed her car over a week ago, and that's why she can't get to work on time, blah, blah, blah. I want to tell them to quit their whining and suck it up, but as their manager, I think more is expected of me." I start to laugh.

"Its times like this, I wish you could have taught me a little bit more about life, Mommy. You know, more about people."

Realizing my bluntness may sound like an accusation, I backtrack. "I'm sorry. It wasn't a criticism. I'm just feeling a little overworked and overwhelmed right now."

I wait for the angry, sarcastic rhetoric to spew from her mouth. Instead, she takes a piece of tangerine from my lap and slowly chews it. There's no arguing, no negating my feelings, no one-upmanship, that if my life was hard, hers was worse. I get a simple nod of recognition with a gesture of her head.

I marvel at this genuine moment of what appears to be her listening to me, hoping that it will continue. A warm, loving exchange most daughters have with their mothers without thought, I've waited decades to receive.

Encouraged by this new medicated parent, I wait before asking her quietly about her relationship with her father, if he had done something to her. She looks up from her lap, gazing at me with neither anger nor hate, just a blank stare. She remains silent.

Oh, God, I did it again. I pushed it too far.

"I'm sorry, Ma. I shouldn't have asked. It wasn't my place."

Her eyes look straight through me, locked in some cobwebbed moment in time. I whisper her name, hoping to bring her back from wherever she is.

She raises a bony finger to her lips and murmurs, "Shh, it's our secret," mimicking an unmistakable flashback I have of my grandfather.

A memory I remember all too well of him approaching me on one of those Sunday nights after a day of drinking, and the overwhelming stench of whiskey on his breath. He bends over saying those very same words, making me believe I was special enough to get that dollar bill he was holding in his hand.

Another piece of my family puzzle clicks into place.

It's true. Oh, God, it's true.

I lose my breath, overcome by the significance of this moment, realizing how a simple gesture can release the dark spirits of the past.

I see my drunk, overbearing grandfather hovering over his young daughter's bed, pressing his menacing finger against her lips. Grandpa is silently threatening her to keep quiet, so his sleeping wife won't hear him playing out his sins in the next room.

Questions begin to loom. Did my grandmother know what he was doing? Is this why my mother didn't like her? Why she had nothing good to say about her? Why didn't my grandmother protect her? Did Nana turn a blind eye? Only my mother knew the answers to those troubling questions. I was left alone to surmise.

I struggle to grasp the enormity of this revelation from my mother's mysterious past, trying to comfort the grey-haired child now emerging from the shadow of her vulnerability. In a hoarse whisper, I tell her how genuinely sorry I am, that I love her. I hug her tightly, holding onto this sacred moment between mother and daughter, vaguely hoping it could be a new beginning.

But soon after our time in the garden, she refused to eat or take her medication. Like those perfect summer days of my youth out on the Long Island Sound, the expectation of a connection was short-lived. Mother would be dead a week later, and the cause of death would be a failure to thrive. The truth about her childhood, however late, found its way toward the light and gave me some consolation.

An Emerging Spirit

T oday, I have the dubious distinction of delivering my mother's eulogy to a small assembly of mourners gathered in the same church as my father. Nervous, I shuffle the prepared notes around the pulpit, hoping to delay the inevitable.

Finding my voice isn't easy. Clichés about the deceased, as a woman, wife, and mother, don't begin to measure the depth or reality of our family's loss and grief.

Mother's polished walnut casket rests in the middle of the church aisle, directly facing the Crucified Christ over the altar. The pallbearers stand like little wooden soldiers next to her, waiting for the bagpiper to finish playing *Amazing Grace*.

Her death is surreal. I can hardly believe she's gone, and yet, I'm relieved to be free from the oppression of being her daughter. People called her Betty. Her formal name was Elizabeth, the same as my middle name. I'm half Joan, half Elizabeth, a mutated epithet that I couldn't fuse to, nor completely disconnect from, in my shaky identity of being her daughter.

My eyes scan the church looking for the small group of AA friends who have protected me against relapsing into that first drink. Weddings and funerals are the common triggers for fledgling recoverees like myself, and I'm grateful for the support of my sponsor, and the other women like Elin K., who opened her home to me during the two-hour dinner break between viewings. Instead of going to the bar with grieving relatives, as I've done in the past, a small group of us went to Elin's house to share stories, laugh, and talk over a platter of assorted sandwiches and soft drinks. First things first, I say to myself.

Hurricane Ike has slammed southeast Texas, leaving all flights canceled, forcing Cathleen and her family to evacuate to Louisiana by car. I want to believe that Divine Providence had something to do with Cathy not being able to attend the funeral. The 'Countess' suffered the most at the hands of our mother, and this unexpected storm might give my sister some time and emotional distance to deal with the death of someone who never showed her any real love.

Timmy sits in the same front pew as he did on the day of my father's funeral. He's with his current family, his wife of six years, a mother-in-law, and a few of their friends. Timmy and I don't have much to say.

My uncle, the priest, who gave the eulogy at my father's funeral, has long since passed.

Work and school schedules have prevented Brian and Brendan from attending their grandmother's funeral. Unbeknownst to all of us, their father will be dead in another week. Bill will die from a sudden heart attack, further tearing the family fabric into unrecognizable threads. My children's lack of understanding of how their father unduly influenced them will take them on their own spiritual journey. I can only hope my sons find the answers they need.

Once again, I wonder if Bill and Betty's dying a week apart is part of God's wisdom or just plain coincidence. Two emotionally damaged people who left behind a legacy of unresolved turmoil and mental illness. Death may have freed them from their chains here on earth, but where do their demons go? Back into the air? Into the unwitting spirits of those who loved them? I have no answers. I'm still working out the trauma inflicted on me. I only know I couldn't fight their darkness against my own. I tried and lost. Now I can only try to understand and forgive them.

I stand alone at the pulpit, waiting for the bagpiper to finish, the signal for those in attendance to know it's time.

"Thank you all for coming today. Elizabeth, but most of you know her as Betty, would have been so pleased to see you all here today, honoring her life here on earth, a life that spanned just over eight decades."

My voice starts to quiver. Something feels wrong. And that familiar 'fight or flight' response begins to rumble inside me. Suddenly, I want to run, but that can't be an option. I'm not sure what I want to say, or what's going to come out of my mouth. I look down at my cheat notes where I scribbled cookies, cigarettes, and the newspaper as my mother's favorite things.

Oh, dear Lord, I'm screwed! Help me.

I take a deep breath looking away from my notes. Seconds pass, maybe minutes. An energy that I recognize as grace comes over me. The fear disappears, allowing me to breathe. I can no longer tolerate the lie that was so much a part of my family. Despite my flawed and wounded nature, God has placed in me the truth. And I must speak it today. I wait for the words to come.

"The dictionary defines the word 'eulogy' as a testimony praising how a deceased person lived and loved. This is difficult for me to say. And maybe, for some of you to hear, but my mother did neither of those two things."

From the front pew, Timmy stares up at me like an angry bull. I take a deep breath, hoping and praying that the right words will come, ignoring my brother's harsh, threatening look.

"My mother was an anomaly. She didn't fit the image that most of us have of moms. She didn't like to cook, bake, or even take care of the household, but fear kept her from doing anything else. She didn't like my father much and liked her daughters even less. My brother Timmy was the only one who could make my mother smile. Timmy was the only one who could make the family appear normal. My mother had what the professionals call narcissism, a mental disorder that prevents a person from being their true self. No one can say for sure how my mother became a narcissist, but this illness kept her from giving and experiencing the real love we had for and wanted from her."

I keep my eyes riveted on the coffin, too afraid to look up and see the shocked look on people's faces.

"It's safe to say I mourned the loss of my mother long before today. Over the last 50 years of my life, I've grieved the moments, hours, and years we would never share as a mother and daughter. I cried more tears when she was alive than I probably will after today."

I take a deep breath, briefly observing the faces of my audience scattered throughout the pews waiting for people to shake their heads and leave. No one does, not even Timmy. I continue.

"Had it not been for my religion and the authority of God's Fourth Commandment, I wouldn't have understood my mother."

I hear the stirring sounds of recognition and feel encouraged to go forward.

"The Bible tells us to honor our mother and father so that we may live long in the land that God gives us."

Wincing up toward the heavens, I say, "I certainly hope my days are long after this eulogy."

I hear a few more chuckles.

"I honored my mother as the person who gave me birth, and took care of her in her last days here on earth, but we had slightly different interpretations of what that commandment meant. She believed in letting the past stay in the past without addressing it. That's fine if the past doesn't disrupt the present. But it did in my mother's case.

In AA, there's a saying, 'You're only as sick as your secrets.' It's a slogan with a lot of truth behind it. Secrets are like ghosts; they haunt people and make them sick. They taunt a person until they get what they want: release and freedom."

I take a deep breath, feeling an inner rush of grace, giving me the courage to continue.

"My mother paid a high price for not freeing her ghosts. We all did. Guilt played a big part in her inner turmoil. Catholic guilt is different than the one that implies genuine wrongdoing. Catholic guilt suggests that we're not allowed to question our parents, teachers, or any other authority figure because God would punish us for doing so. The message that we don't have the right to speak up for ourselves even when we're telling the truth gets grossly distorted, and creates more lost souls than redeemed ones."

I nod toward the crucifix on the altar.

"I don't think the Man on the Cross would have agreed with my mother's way of thinking. It negates the purpose of His death and resurrection, which is all about giving us new life, truth, and inner freedom -- not the shackles that guilt and shame create."

The look on some of the faces are expressionless, and others say I've struck a chord. Timmy is no longer giving me dirty looks, so I continue.

"A wise and healing woman taught me a lot about shame. She said that shame is a primitive emotion, a silent killer, so internalized in us that most times, we're not even aware it exists. It cripples the human psyche and dictates most of our choices in life. Shame has a life of its own and gets handed down from one generation to the next. She said that shame-based families are high-stressed, addictive people who always seem to be operating in survivor mode, describing my family to a T."

My brother gives me a nod of recognition. I take deep, measured breaths waiting for the words, not sure what to say next. For some odd reason, old Mrs. Jamison from that spiritual retreat comes to mind.

"Years ago, I remember Mommy telling another woman that Jesus loves everyone. It was His job. I remember thinking to myself, geez, she's comparing Our Lord to a civil servant employee, just doing his job! In her mind, I knew she believed it. She saw Jesus as a man who once lived but had nothing to do with her present-day life and religion. A remote figure built on obligation. For a long time, I believed it too. I know each of us interprets the meaning of God and His Son through our own eyes, beliefs, and life experiences, so please forgive me if you think I'm preaching. It's not my intent.

Today, I know and believe in my heart that Jesus is alive and respects the choices we make. He doesn't barge into our life like some uninvited guest. He waits for our heart and soul to be ready to want Him. Sometimes we call out to Him in need. He doesn't care what our motives are. When we knock, Jesus always responds. And when that door opens, no one is ever disappointed. It comes with a luminous light full of love, healing, and possibilities, alerting us to another way of living, to our potential, and giving us a divine love so powerful and unconditional that it can heal all our wounds. His Holy Love is the only force powerful enough to heal us from the darkness of our inner shame – our own and that which others thrust upon us. I only wish my mom understood this when she was alive. But, I believe she does now."

I look over at the casket and feel the tears well up in me.

"Your war is over, Mommy. Rest in peace."

www.ingramcontent.com/pod-product-compliance
Lightning Source LLC
Chambersburg PA
CBHW051722040426
42447CB00008B/933